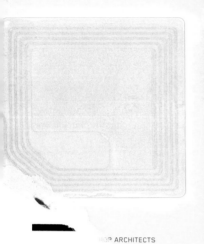

QUINZE AND MILAN

ARCHITECTS

university college
for the creative arts

ZENKAYA

SHIGERU BAN ARCHITECTS

D1612360

OSA OFFICE FOR SUBVERSIVE ARCHITECTURE

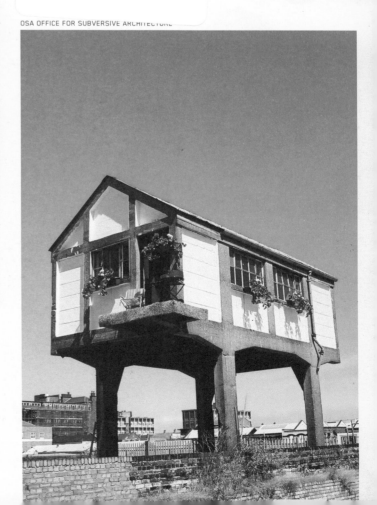

SPACE
CRAFT

FLEETING ARCHITECTURE
AND HIDEOUTS

EDITED BY ROBERT KLANTEN AND LUKAS FEIREISS
DIE GESTALTEN VERLAG

CONTENT

CONTRIBUTORS

./STUDIO3 – INSTITUTE FOR EXPERIMENTAL ARCHITECTURE
24H ARCHITECTURE
3DELUXE
AKIRA SUZUKI / WORKSHOP FOR ARCHITECTURE AND URBANISM
AB ROGERS
ADAM KALKIN
ALCHEMY ARCHITECTS
ALEXANDER BRODSKY
ALRIK KOUDENBURG
ANDREA ZITTEL
ANDY HOLDEN
AOC ARCHITECTURE LTD.
APRÈS-NOUS
ARNO BRANDLHUBER
ART LEAGUE HOUSTON
ATELIER BOW-WOW
ATELIER HITOSHI ABE
ATELIER KEMPE THILL
ATELIER OPA
ATELIER TEKUTO
ATELIER VAN LIESHOUT
B&K+ BRANDLHUBER & KNIESS
BAKERYGROUP
BARNSTORMERS
BARRY MCGEE
BAUBOTANIK
BAUMRAUM
BERT NEUMANN / LSD BERLIN

BILD DESIGN
COLLEGE OF ENVIRONMENTAL DESIGN
COMPLIZEN PLANUNGSBÜRO
DADARA
DANIEL DILGER, MARC OSWALD, NIKLAS SCHECHINGER AND HANK SCHMIDT IN DER BEEK
DAVID GREENBERG
DE MARIA DESIGN ASSOCIATES INC.
DETROIT COLLABORATIVE DESIGN CENTER
DE VIJF B.V. / SPACEBOX
DILLER SCOFIDIO + RENFRO
DIONISIO GONZÁLEZ
DIRETRIBE
DO-HO SUH
DRÉ WAPENAAR
EARTHSHIP BIOTECTURE
EDOUARD FRANCOIS
ELECTROLAND LLC
ENCORE HEUREUX
ERWIN WURM
ETOY.CORPORATION
EXILHÄUSER ARCHITEKTEN
EXYZT
FARM DESIGN
FELD72
FLORENTIJN HOFMAN
FNP ARCHITEKTEN
FOLKE KÖBBERLING & MARTIN KALTWASSER

FRANKA HÖRNSCHEMEYER
FRANK HAVERMANS
FREE SPIRIT SPHERES
FRIEDRICH VON BORRIES, TOBIAS NEUMANN
GAGAT INTERNATIONAL
GELITIN
GIANCARLO NORESE
GIN JOHANNES
GRAFFITI RESEARCH LAB
GRÜNTUCH ERNST ARCHITEKTEN
GRUPPO A12
HANS SCHABUS
HAWORTH TOMPKINS
HEATHERWICK STUDIO
HEXENKESSEL & STRAND GMBH
HORDEN CHERRY LEE ARCHITECTS & LYDIA HAACK AND
JOHN HÖPFNER ARCHITEKTEN
HÜTTEN & PALÄSTE ARCHITEKTEN
HYPERBODY RESEARCH GROUP
INTERBREEDING FIELD
ISLAND AMBIANCE
IVAN KROUPA ARCHITECTS
JAN DE COCK
JENSKE DIJKHUIS
JESKO FEZER / MATHIAS HEYDEN
JOHANNES KAUFMANN ARCHITEKTUR
KENGO KUMA & ASSOCIATES
KLAUS STATTMANN
KORTEKNIE STUHLMACHER ARCHITECTEN
KREISSL KERBER
LAB(AU) I LABORATORY FOR ARCHITECTURE AND URBANISM
LANG/BAUMANN
LEONARD VAN MUNSTER
LOCO ARCHITECTS
LOT-EK
LUIS RAFAEL BERRÍOS-NEGRÓN
M-HOUSE
MAD HOUSERS
MARIA PADADIMITRIU
MARJETICA POTRČ
MARTTI KALLIALA AND ESA RUSKEEPÄÄ WITH MARTIN LUKASCYZK
MATEJ ANDRAŽ VOGRINIČIČ
MATIAS CREIMER
MATS KARLSSON
MAURER UNITED ARCHITECTS [MUA]
MEIXNER SCHLÜTER WENDT ARCHITEKTEN
MICHAEL ELMGREEN / INGAR DRAGSET
MICHAEL JANTZEN
MICHAEL RAKOWITZ
MICHAEL SAILSTORFER
MIKAN ARCHITECTS
MIKE MEIRÉ
MMW ARCHITECTS OF NORWAY
MODULORBEAT
NARCHITECTS
NATHALIE WOLBERG
NATHAN COLEY
NILS HOLGER MOORMANN
NOHOTEL
NOMAD HOME TRADING GMBH
NONCON:FORM
ODA PROJESI
OLAFUR ELIASSON

OMD – OFFICE OF MOBILE DESIGN
ONL (OOSTERHUIS_LÉNÁRD)
OPTREKTRANSVAAL
OSA OFFICE FOR SUBVERSIVE ARCHITECTURE
PARSONS THE NEW SCHOOL FOR DESIGN / ST. ETIENNE SCHOOL
OF ART AND DESIGN / KONSTFACK UNIVERSITY OF COLLEGE OF
ARTS, CRAFT AND DESIGN
PATKAU ARCHITECTS
PEANUTZ ARCHITEKTEN
PETER FATTINGER, VERONIKA ORSO, MICHAEL RIEPER
PLASTIQUE FANTASTIQUE
PLATOON . CULTURAL DEVELOPMENT
PPAG ARCHITECTS
PRIMITIVO SUAREZ-WOLFE
PUBLIC ARCHITECTURE
QUINZE AND MILAN
R&SIE(N)
RAUMLABOR BERLIN
RAUMTAKTIK
REALITIES:UNITED
REBAR
RECETAS URBANAS
REISER + UMEMOTO
RICCARDO PREVIDI
RICHARD WILSON
RO&AD ARCHITECTEN
ROBBRECHT EN DAEM ARCHITECTEN
ROB VOERMAN
RONAN & ERWAN BOUROULLEC
SEAN GODSELL ARCHITECTS
SHAHRAM ENTEKHABI
SHE_ARCHITEKTEN
SHIGERU BAN ARCHITECTS
SHOP ARCHITECTS
SIMON STARLING
STEALTH.UNLIMITED
STEFAN EBERSTADT
STEFAN EICHHORN
STEVEN HOLL ARCHITECTS
STUDIO AISSLINGER
STUDIO MAKKINK & BEY BV
STUDIO NL-D
STUDIO ROOSEGAARDE
T.O.P. OFFICE
TAZRO NISCINO
TERUNOBU FUJIMORI
TERUNOBU FUJIMORI AND NOBUMICHI OHSIMA (OSHIMA ATELIER)
THE CHAPUISAT BROTHERS
THE SNOW SHOW
THOMAS BRATZKE
THOMAS DEMAND
TODD SAUNDERS AND TOMMIE WILHELMSEN
TOM SACHS
TROIKA
ULRIKE MYRZIK AND MANFRED JARISCH
UCHRONIA
URBAN SPACE MANAGEMENT LTD.
USMAN HAQUE (HAQUE DESIGN + RESEARCH)
VALESKA PESCHKE
VAZIO S/A ARQUITETURA E URBANISMO
WEXLER STUDIO
WOLFGANG WINTER + BERHOLD HOERBELT
ZENKAYA

SPACECRAFT

FLEETING ARCHITECTURE AND HIDEOUTS
LUKAS FEIREISS

Like a giant breaking wave frozen in time and space, a breathtaking construction from innumerable timber beams rises as high as a house above the desert only, to collapse in flames at the moment of its completion to the accompanying dizzy rejoicing of its creators. Detached from its surroundings, a patinated metal box appears like a stranded ark. Away from the urban tumult, this reduced building, standing alone out on the open plain, seems to allude to archaic structural archetypes. Erupting blisters of space burst out from beneath motorway bridges and create intriguing sites of cultural conviviality. In scenes of Babylonian audacity, camper vans, scaffolding and strip lights are piled up into a neck-breaking tower that reaches way above the treetops. Elegant, amorphous architectures emerge out of ice, and a rough freight container folds open to reveal a snug place of contemplation decorated with wood panelling and chandeliers.

Each of these various projects conveys just a taste of the intense and diverse language of space demonstrated by the works presented in this book. In their poetic eccentricity, they are expressions of a shifting, multi-dimensional understanding of architecture and space. The discipline of space creation has long since ceased to be the exclusive domain of architects. For many creatives it has now become an emotionally charged expression of their urge for originality in spatial structures. This of course means that architects are losing their traditional sovereign right to the formal design of buildings/spaces, but it is precisely in the overthrow of established etiquette in our built surroundings that the unique chance arises to discover new and fascinating space worlds.

The standard definition of space is length x width x height. But spatial design is much more than simply dealing with the entirety of three-dimensionally defined objects in relationship to one another and to discerning subjects in Euclidian space: it is the primordial scenario of architecture and a basic prerequisite for man's exploration of his world.

Thus space as the subject of serious discussion opens horizons of meaning that inevitably go way beyond the scope and intentions of this book, which lives first and foremost through its many images. The selected projects are playfully topological in nature: they are radical spatial investigations. Here adventurous and provocative examples of the creative crafting of spaces beyond the mainstream are traced with great passion and curiosity. A rich seam of imagination and ideas has been tapped, revealing the hidden potential of contemporary spatial production modes and opening up perspectives into a magical world of diversity. The title alone indicates the complexity of practices. With its intentional double meaning, Spacecraft creates a bridge between the grounded, solid craftsmanship of building and the conquering of gravity through space travel towards the 'final frontiers' – the ultimate projection of all that is new and unknown. To continue the metaphor, the primary mission of this book, in its essential and stalwart examination of 'space', is to "explore strange new worlds."

With a joyful sense of discovery, this book documents numerous experimental positions from a range of very different disciplinary and cultural contexts, which highlight an inspiring extension of the standard definitions of space in architecture, art and design. Stimulating structures are presented that break original and new ground in the understanding of building practices. The desire for new space is palpable in all of them. They all radiate a refreshing spirit of change. At the same time they are an expression of wide-ranging social developments – since built space is also cultural space and a mirror of its time.

In the presence of changes in all areas of contemporary life through increased, social and cultural mobility, and ubiquitous networking via communication and information technologies, our living and working spaces are confronted with new, previously unimagined challenges. In their pro-active nature as autonomously functioning 'buildings', many of the works shown here are highly appropriate to the demands for increased flexibility and plurality resulting from these changes. Interestingly though, many of the works also appear to be anachronisms in the face of the dissolution of conventional architectural terms in the virtual worlds of the digital age. The extremely material nature of the building materials and shapes is especially sensually tangible in these projects. It seems as if – through their intense preoccupation with the physical presence and haptic qualities of architecture and space – they are somehow trying to work against being absorbed into the world of the virtual image.

Although we usually understand architecture to be a statically fixed discipline where objects are generally built to last, the process-like nature of many of the projects shown here are united in their impermanence. Thus the poetical paradox contained in the book's subtitle Fleeting Architecture covers the surprising variation and bandwidth featured here whilst focusing clearly on the ephemeral nature of many of the works. While going beyond the usual categorisation of temporary architectural spaces, as simply those with flexible occupation and time-limited usage, this publication also recognises a diversity of distinctive hideouts that can be used temporarily or seasonally. Whereas the first category covers spaces such as pavilions, art projects and cultural spaces that are only lived in for a short period of time, the second category represents permanent refuges such as ateliers, offices, tree houses or holiday homes that are resided in sporadically yet repeatedly.

With reference to the phenomenon 'dwelling', the projects clearly reflect at times conflicting patterns in human experience. On the one hand is the apparent dialectic between man's need for stability and his compulsion for change and to modify his surroundings. At first glance, this static need for security seems directly opposed to the desire for dynamic progress. But when one considers the historically deeply anchored nomadic nature of man, then the discrepancy is only apparent since, in terms of human history, living in statically fixed environments tends to be the exception rather than the rule. The creation of flexible, mobile architecture, then, appears to unite mankind's ancient, conflicting basic needs. However, in their progression to extremes, the projects also primarily exemplify the immutable and all too human desire for uniquely individual habitations. Space concerns all of us and the spaces that we construct and live in are always an expression of ourselves.

The kaleidoscopic spectrum of motivations that lie behind the works presented here is a direct reflection of the creative wealth involved in constructing spatial possibilities. They all play their part in the continuous renewal of our environment and extend from aesthetically demanding art projects to practical family homes via performative models of space occupation and socially motivated constructions. In the choice of projects from Africa, Australia, Asia, Europe and America, emphasis was placed on thematic diversity and presenting particularly accomplished examples. The same applies to the categories selected, which distinguish the projects from one another but are at the same time principally open and even invite reciprocal exchange.

The chapter Off Track presents spaces that disconnect themselves from defined living units and prescribed locations. They are dwellings beyond the beaten track of architecture, boltholes and escapes, often in extreme settings, that are situated away from the bustle of urban life or satisfy the desire for increased mobility.

With specific examples, Modular extends the theme of mobile homes into the vast field of possibilities related to modular building elements such as containers, boxes and the like.

Over the Top is dedicated to surprising add-ons to existing building structures and a variety of, often ironic, vertical extensions in city and rural areas. New living and working spaces are to be found here, from urban rooftop developments to tree houses located far away from civilisation.

Shanty Town is inspired by the informal building and settlement formats common to many developing countries. The projects shown here combine the dynamic eclecticism of their subversive design mandate beyond standard blueprint mechanisms and cover ancient hut-like buildings as well as three-dimensional space collages made from apparently trivial everyday materials.

Showtime is the theme of the final chapter, which addresses performative spaces within the art world. An intriguing collection of hybrids are to be found here whose attention is focused on the dramaturgical and scenical effects of space. The chapter covers works that are purely artistic as well as media-inspired space enhancements and active participatory practices in alternative space occupation.

In its vitality, this book is intended to be an intoxicating compendium of spatial curiosities that inspire intensive reflection as well as imitation. Since space, as mentioned at the beginning, represents a prominent aspect of man's existential nature, it is hoped that this book does not just reach out to architects alone. It has been my explicit intention to create a source of inspiration for creatives across all disciplines, to encourage the individual design of spaces as a fruitful and rewarding field of activity. I hope that the personal enthusiasm that has gripped me in the exploration of architecture and spaces in general — and particularly during the development of this book — will spread to the reader, who is then equally piqued, moved and even vexed. In recognition of the remarkable perspectives that contemporary spatial practices have opened up, Spacecraft affords readers a view of totally unexpected zones of action and possibility and invites them to take flight on a tour de force through new spatial and conceptual worlds.

So buckle up and enjoy the ride!

ZENKAYA

ATELIER TEKUTO

OFF TRACK

This opening chapter presents spaces that have slipped the bonds of standard living models and prescribed locations. They are dwellings that are found beyond architecture's beaten track, places of escape and calm – often in extreme settings situated away from the whirl of city life, or mobile shelters that answer to the demands of increased mobility. The discussion generated by such specific living structures is also always very revealing in regard to social structures. In recent years, political and economical internationalisation, rapid technological innovation and cultural changes have triggered great leaps in the nature of mobility, flexibility and acceleration in all niches of modern life, particularly in the closely linked areas of living and working.

These selected projects satisfy the attendant demands on contemporary living space that arise from such changes in a variety of ways. For example, Michael Reynold's futuristic Earthships built out of car tyres and Alchemy Architects' weeHouses, which seem disconnected from their surroundings, or Steven Holl's silver Turbulence House on the New Mexico mesa, all offer autonomous sites of contemplation and peace far from all forms of civilisation.

Other exemplary projects, including Atelier Tekuto's Lucky Drop house elegantly inserted into a side street, or Nathalie Wolberg's presentation of a playful studio conversion, demonstrate that it is possible to provide intimate shelters within the city as well. There are also creative suggestions for problems related to migration to urban areas: working together with a local community in southern Italy, the architect team feld72 have realised a successful example of participatory revitalisation with their Million Donkey Hotel in an abandoned medieval village centre.

Alongside all these idiosyncratic dwellings you will also find nomadic abodes presented in all their creative diversity. From the ethereal shimmer of Ronan and Erwan Bouroullec's pragmatically poetic habitable barge gliding down the river to Atelier van Lieshout's floating sculpture that metastizes an old houseboat way out into the blue.

Dré Wappenaar, MIKAN Architects and the Office for Subversive Architecture construct fascinating tent camps in a variety of colours and complexities, and Valeska Peschke inflates her transportable Instant Home within minutes in apparently uninhabitable locations. But this is just the beginning!

The works shown here present new concepts and ideas for the construction of relatively small, flexible and usable spaces that accommodate the desire for a nomadic life and unlimited mobility on the one hand, and permit freedom to build and live according to individual needs on the other. Thus they are roaming freely beyond the paved routes of conventional architecture.

DRÉ WAPENAAR

IVAN KROUPA ARCHITECTS
Ivan Kroupa, Radka Exnerová

SNOWBOARDERS' COTTAGE
Herlikovice, Czech Republic, 2001

ZENKAYA
Eric Bigot

ZENKAYA
South Africa, 2006

M-HOUSE
Tim Pyne

M-HOUSE
Canterbury, United Kingdom, 2002

**HORDEN CHERRY LEE ARCHITECTS AND
LYDIA HAACK + JOHN HÖPFNER ARCHITEKTEN**

MICRO COMPACT HOME
Munich, Germany 2005

The Micro Compact Home by Horden Cherry
Lee Architects and Lydia Haack + John Höpfner
Architekten is a transportable, lightweight
aluminium cube, specifically designed for short-
stay smart living and suitable for a variety of
locations. It provides sophisticated compact
accommodation for business or leisure use.
All mod cons are integrated, including furniture, sound, flat-screen, communication and
energy systems.

ALCHEMY ARCHITECTS

<u>WEEHOUSE</u>
Marfa, USA, 2006

ALCHEMY ARCHITECTS

<u>WEEHOUSE</u>
Pepin, USA, 2003

TODD SAUNDERS AND
TOMMIE WILHELMSEN

SUMMER HOUSE
Hardanger Fjord, Norway, 2003

OMD – OFFICE OF MOBILE DESIGN
Jennifer Siegal

SEATRAIN RESIDENCE
The Brewery, Los Angeles, 2003

In this residential complex for a living and working artists' community in Los Angeles, industrial and traditional materials – including storage containers and steel found on site in downtown L.A. – are playfully combined. This home and work space literally grows out of the land around it, engaging with and incorporating its industrial history. Here, recycled materials are not just practical and cost-effective; they create a unique, dramatic architectural vocabulary.

JOHANNES KAUFMANN ARCHITEKTUR
Johannes Kaufmann

SU–SI
Reuthe, Austria, 1998

JOHANNES KAUFMANN ARCHITEKTUR
Johannes Kaufmann

FRED
Dornbirn, Austria, 1999

STUDIO AISSLINGER
Werner Aisslinger

LOFTCUBE
Milan, Italy, 2007

NOMAD HOME TRADING GMBH
Gerod Peham

NOMAD HOME
Seekirchen, Austria, 2006

NATHALIE WOLBERG

MAISON ATELIER À SAINT-OUEN
Paris, France, 2004

AB ROGERS
Ab Rogers with Shona Kitchen

page 16/17 |
KENNY SCHACHTER HOUSE
London, United Kingdom, 2004

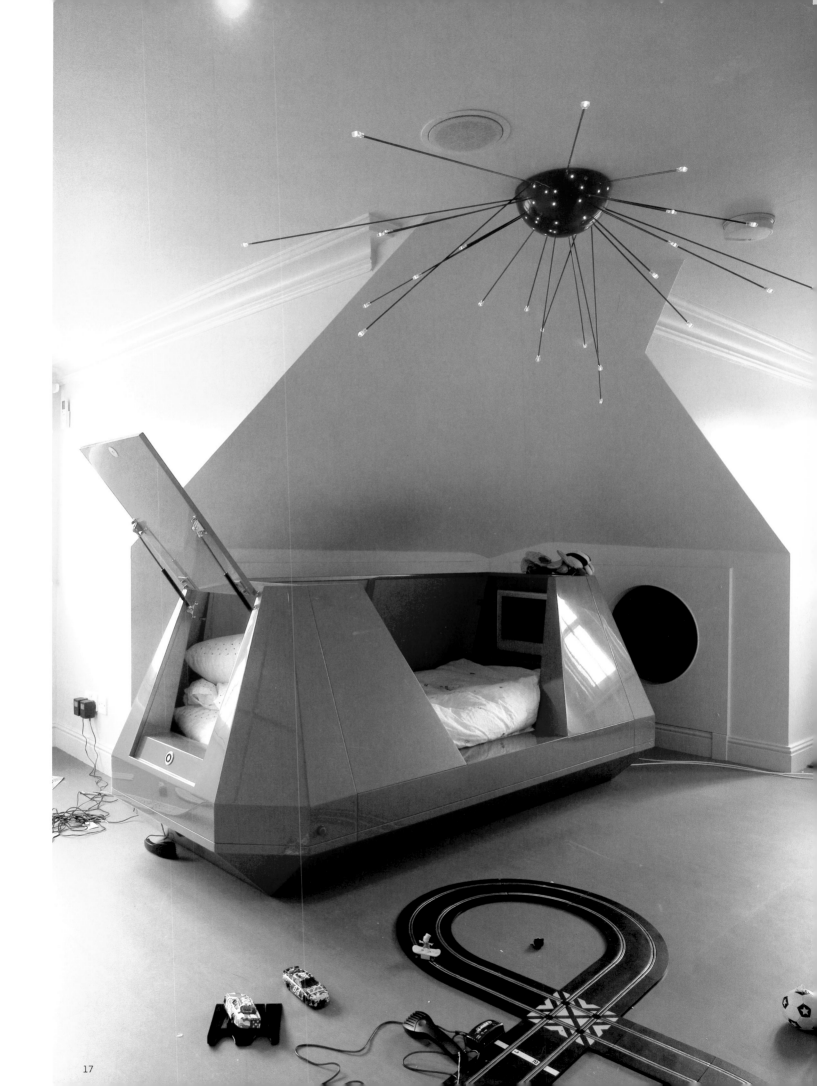

ATELIER VAN LIESHOUT
Joep van Lieshout

FLOATING SCULPTURE
Amsterdam, Netherlands, 2000

Rotterdam-based Atelier Van Lieshout is a multidisciplinary company that operates internationally in the field of contemporary art, design and architecture. Their work includes sculptures, furniture, bathrooms and mobile home units as well as complete architectural refurbishments. Amongst the many application forms and techniques used by Atelier van Lieshout are their large polyester constructions in striking, bright colours.

The longer side of Floating Sculpture is based on the old-fashioned architecture of a Zaans huisje (a housing style found in the Zaanstreek, an old industrial district in northern Holland). The attached blue bulb with windows has a large round bed inside. While providing living comforts afloat, the sculpture can also be used as a koek & zoopie bar – a Dutch term for a place that serves hot chocolate and snacks to ice skaters gliding across the frozen canals in winter.

STUDIO MAKKINK & BEY BV
Jurgen Bey

BLOB (BINARY LARGE OBJECT)
Eindhoven, Netherlands, 2004

ATELIER TEKUTO
Yasuhiro Yamashita (Atelier Tekuto) with
Masahiro Ikeda (Masahiro Ikeda Co.,Ltd)

LUCKY DROPS
Setagaya, Tokyo, 2005

In shape and size this house by Tokyo-based architect Yasuhiro Yamashita's Atelier Tekuto stands out amongst the numerous houses designed for small plots of land in Japan. The building takes advantage of the site's narrow dimensions by ensuring a maximum length of the building; providing a space for fun and structural reinforcement to the building by introducing a slope inside; making the best use of underground space and turning the entire building into a skin. The above-ground section features skin-like external walls with added transparency, letting sunlight permeate the entire building. The floor material is expanded metal, letting sunlight reach further underground.

RAUMLABOR BERLIN
Benjamin Foerster-Baldinius

FNP ARCHITEKTEN

MILLION DONKEY HOTEL
Prata Sannita, Italy, 2005 – 2006

The Million Donkey Hotel by the Viennese architecture office feld72, built in cooperation with a local community in Southern Italy, addresses one of the big challenges of this region: migration and its consequences. International artists were invited to the Matese Regional Parc to create (art) projects in collaboration with the local population that focus on the relationship between identity, territory and social space.

feld72 saw new potential for the future in the abandoned spaces of the medieval village of Prata Sannita. The project interconnects disparate elements into one big interactive space. Four of these lost spaces in the town centre were transformed into inhabitable installations with the help of the locals. Thus the Million Donkey Hotel was the beginning of a re-activation of some forgotten parts of the village and an expansion of its public space. It is run by an association of volunteers; visitors can just look around or book rooms.

KENGO KUMA & ASSOCIATES
Kengo Kuma

GREAT (BAMBOO) WALL
Bejing, China, 2002

AOC ARCHITECTURE LTD.

FOLLY FOR A FILMMAKER
Hertfordshire, United Kingdom, 2004

R&SIE(N)
Francois Roche, Phillipe Parreno

HYBRID MUSCLE
Chan Mai, Thailand, 2002

As part of The Land – a project that merges ideas by different artists and architects from all over the world to create a place of social engagement in the Thai village of Sanpatong – R&Sie(n) constructed a work and exhibition space that would generate its own electricity from the work of animals. Mechanical energy was converted into electrical energy through the lifting of a two-ton steel counterweight by an albino buffalo and then used to power light bulbs, laptops and cell phones.

STEVEN HOLL ARCHITECTS

TURBULENCE HOUSE
New Mexico, USA, 2004

EARTHSHIP BIOTECTURE
Michael Reynolds

New Mexico, USA, 2004–2006

Earthship Biotecture, based in Taos, New Mexico and founded by architect and engineer Michael Reynolds, creates passive solar homes made of natural and recycled materials that function completely independently and self-sufficiently. "Earthships heat and cool themselves naturally via solar/thermal dynamics, collect their own power from the sun and wind, harvest their own water from rain and snow melt, contain and treat their own sewage on site, produce food in significant quantities and utilise materials that are by-products of modern society - such as cans, bottles and tyres," says Reynolds.

SEAN GODSELL ARCHITECTS

FUTURE SHACK
Melbourne, Australia, 2001

The Future Shack by Australian architect Sean Godsell is a mass-produced mobile house for emergency and relief housing. Recycled shipping containers are used to form the main volume of the building. A parasol roof packs inside the container. When erected, the roof shades the container and reduces heat load on the building. Legs telescope from the container enabling it to be sited without excavation on uneven terrain. The universal nature of the container means that the houses can be stockpiled and easily transported throughout the world. The Future Shack can be fully erected in 24 hours.

ATELIER VAN LIESHOUT
Joep van Lieshout

MINI CAPSULE FRONT ENTRANCE
Amsterdam, Netherlands, 2000

The Mini Capsule Front Entrance is designed to be used as an unmanned budget hotel and offers two guests the bare minimum of comfort. The interior is not much larger than a double bed and is equipped with the basics: just a mattress, sheets, blankets, a nightlight, clothing hooks and electricity. The front entrance version cannot be stacked; each unit stands on four legs just above the ground.

ANDREA ZITTEL

A–Z HOMESTEAD UNIT FROM A–Z WEST
California, USA, 2003

A–Z WAGON STATION
California, USA, 2003

Since 2000, the Californian artist Andrea Zittel has been working at A–Z West in the California desert to develop a body of work that addresses contemporary perceptions of freedom and personal liberation.

"It is my theory that personal liberation is now achieved through individual attempts to 'slip between the cracks'. Instead of building big ranches and homesteads, today's independence seekers prefer small portable structures, which evade the regulatory control of bureaucratic restrictions."

SPA FOR AIR AND LIGHT
Frankfurt / Main, Germany, 2003

The Spa for Air and Light by Frankfurt architects Meixner Schlüter Wendt is a concept for a floating building situated on a peninsula in the Main river in Frankfurt, Germany.
During the winter, the park containing the peninsula is closed to the public due to high water levels and flooding. During the summer, the 'spa' building serves as a restaurant and snack bar with a 'driftwood terrace' in front of it. In the winter the stairs are folded up, the building closes up and floats on the water to hibernate through the cold season.

KORTEKNIE STUHLMACHER ARCHITECTEN

<u>HOUSE NO 19 – MOBILE STUDIO FOR ARTISTS</u>
Utrecht, Netherlands, 2003

RONAN & ERWAN BOUROULLEC

FLOATING HOUSE
Chatou, France, 2006

ATELIER OPA
Toshihiko Suzuki

<u>THE MOBILE CHA-NO-YU ROOM</u>
Tokyo, Japan, 2000

The Mobile Cha-no-yu Room by Japanese architect Toshihiko Suzuki's Atelier OPA was created as spatial product between furniture and architecture. As with most of Suzuki's work, furniture is somehow designed as space and space as product.

PATKAU ARCHITECTS

LA PETITE MAISON DU WEEKEND
Vancouver, Canda, 1999

La Petite Maison du Weekend by Canadian architects Patkau is a prototype for a self-sufficient dwelling. Intended as minimal accommodation for a weekend getaway for two, it can be located on virtually any outdoor site, including remote, unserviced locations, and provides the basics for everyday life: shelter, sleeping loft, kitchen, shower and toilet. The building furthermore generates its own electricity, collects and distributes rainwater, and composts waste using only the natural dynamics of the site.

EXILHÄUSER ARCHITEKTEN

ZUSATZRAUM – OFFICE FOR ANYWHERE
Germany, 2000

NOHOTEL
Tobias Lehmann, Floris Schiferli

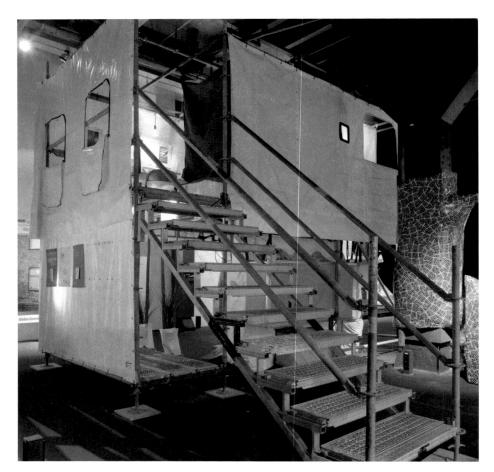

BAKERYGROUP
Marcin Padlewski, Anissa Szeto

SOFT CLINIC
Ontario, Canada, 2002

SOFT CLINIC
Ontario, Canada, 2002

Soft Clinic by the Canadian Bakerygroup was designed for a mobile AIDS/HIV clinic competition organized by Architecture for Humanity – a charitable organization that promotes architectural and design solutions to global, social and humanitarian crises. Soft Clinic is a fully integrated, folding tensile structure and self-contained tented enclosure.

The central core of the clinic is used for transportation, storage of equipment, utilities and the tensile enclosure. Minimal cost and ease of fabrication were the principal design criteria. The underlying idea of the Soft Clinic was to develop a structure that could be easily assembled with locally available materials and skills such as fabrics and sewing. The design of the Soft Clinic does not require any special tools or a difficult setup process. Hardware and joinery are simplified by using flexible tubing.

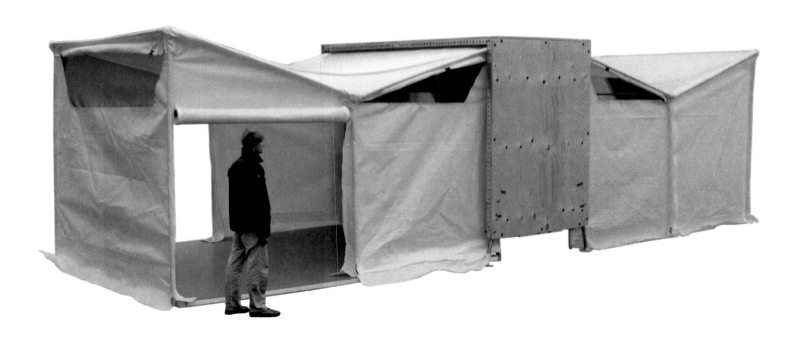

ALRIK KOUDENBURG

BOOM TENT
Netherlands, 2001

DRÉ WAPENAAR

1 | **TREE TENTS**
Rotterdam, Netherlands, 1998
2 | **TENT VILLAGE**
Netherlands, 2001
3 | **BAAR TENT**
Rotterdam, Netherlands, 2003

MICHAEL RAKOWITZ

PARASITE

1 | New York, USA, 2000
2 | Cambridge / Boston, USA, 1998

The paraSITES by American artist Michael Rakowitz are custom-built inflatable shelters designed for homeless people that attach to the exterior outtake vents of a building's heating, ventilation and air-conditioning system. The warm air leaving the building simultaneously inflates and heats the double membrane structure. The paraSITES were distributed to over 30 homeless people in Boston and Cambridge, MA and New York City.

VALESKA PESCHKE

The Instant Home by Berlin-based artist Valeska Peschke travels packed in a simple box and takes only two minutes to inflate into a pitched-roof house complete with furniture. Instant Home was set up in locations typically considered uninhabitable, from city parking lots and suburban driveways to the deserts of the western United States.

1 | **ELEFAN(T)**
Budapest, Hungary, 2003
2 | **MINIFAN(T)**
Bejing, China, 2004

**AKIRA SUZUKI / WORKSHOP FOR
ARCHITECTURE AND URBANISM**

1 | **SELFBUILD SHELTER WORKSHOP**
Kobe, Japan, 2005
2 | **NEWSPAPER HOUSE**
Tokyo, Japan, 2004

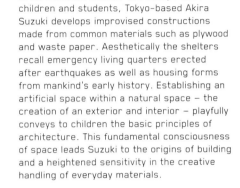

In his Selfbuild Shelter workshops with
children and students, Tokyo-based Akira
Suzuki develops improvised constructions
made from common materials such as plywood
and waste paper. Aesthetically the shelters
recall emergency living quarters erected
after earthquakes as well as housing forms
from mankind's early history. Establishing an
artificial space within a natural space – the
creation of an exterior and interior – playfully
conveys to children the basic principles of
architecture. This fundamental consciousness
of space leads Suzuki to the origins of building
and a heightened sensitivity in the creative
handling of everyday materials.

RAUMTAKTIK
post theater, Matthias Böttger,
Max Schumacher

MATCHMAKER MATCHMAKER
Berlin, Germany, 2003

OSA OFFICE FOR SUBVERSIVE ARCHITECTURE

<u>CAMPINSKI</u>
Frankfurt / Main, Germany, 2005

As part of a four-day workshop at the Darmstadt University of Technology, students were asked to transform a predominantly industrial harbour area via precise interventions in the existing building structure using only simple igloo tents.

DE MARIA DESIGN ASSOCIATES INC.

MODULAR

The following projects deal in a variety of ways with the infinite field of possibilities related to modular building elements. Containers, boxes and other flexible room/space modules serve as raw material for stimulating spatial structures which, in their creative transformation of the notion of prefab systems, establish their own brand of poetry beyond any form of categorisation.

Thus, for example, Adam Kulkin's Push Button House opens up like a flower to reveal a carefully decorated interior of patrician elegance that is in stark contrast to the external appearance of its freight container. There is a similar iconic tension in Luc Deleu's urban installations that show the confrontation between architectural archetypes – such as triumphal arches, obelisks and bridges – and the banal aesthetics of containers. In their playful interaction with cargo containers, the works of Shigeru Ban, Platoon, etoy and raumtaktik emphasise their potential as multifunctional building blocks for a variety of event and exhibition spaces, whereas the 'domestic' buildings of Jennifer Siegal, Lot-ek, De Maria Design and Urban Space Management reveal an extraordinary variety of potential aesthetic possibilities with living containers. All in all, the works shown here clearly emphasise that the flexibility of the cargo container module – as an internationally available, universal object and icon of world trade and modern logistics – allows it to be infinitely mobilised, manipulated and transformed.

But not all the projects in this chapter relate to the container as a component-oriented building unit. Numerous other playful forms of modular architecture are presented here whose scope ranges from flexible city furniture to extendable building structures. The oversized, and endlessly combinable, room elements from PPAG in the Vienna Museum Quarter, the non-dogmatic urban installations from She_Architekten, and Maurer United Architects' exhibition system developed from the computer game Tetris are also examples of modular building. So too the interlocking spatial structures developed by students at the Pasadena City College together with Matias Creimer, or the Little Houses on the Black River, developed in Sweden as part of a trans-university workshop, which are on moveable tracks.

Despite their modular, prefabricated construction, these projects are all distinguished by an incredibly high level of individuality and variability. Together they convey to the reader an impression of the rich and diverse language of form generated from system units that can be seen in modular building today.

PPAG ARCHITECTS

ADAM KALKIN

PUSH BUTTON HOUSE
New York, USA, 2005

Radical American architect and artist Adam Kalkin designed the Push Button House for Art Basel Miami Beach in 2005. It is a shipping container that transforms into a house at the push of a button. Motorised walls unfold, revealing a fully functional house, complete with refined furnishings.

ETOY.CORPORATION

ETOY.TANKS
Worldwide, since 1998

Since 1998 the international etoy team has been working with a standardised cargo container transportation network that covers more than 80% of all freight-forwarding activities on planet Earth. The legendary orange etoy.TANKS are customized cargo containers. In recent years, the multifunctional etoy.TANKS have become a crucial factor in the etoy.GESAMTKUNSTWERK. As independent showrooms, offices, studios, walk-in Web servers and sculptural elements they have been part of international exhibitions, festivals and gallery shows all around the globe.

T.O.P. OFFICE
Luc Deleu

1 | Antwerp, Belgium, 2003
2 | Yokohama, Japan, 2005

This Belgian architect and artist has been making temporary installations in public spaces for more than two decades. He regularly uses cargo containers to construct architectural archetypes, such as the triumphal arch or the cross, that create an ironic tension between the archetypal form and the material used to construct it.

T.O.P. OFFICE
Luc Deleu

3 | Alkmaar, Netherlands, 2006
4 | Nauerna, Netherlands, 2002
5 | Antwerp, Belgium, 2004

RAUMTAKTIK
Friedrich von Borries, Matthias Böttger

FANSHOP OF GLOBALIZATION
Germany, 2006

Before and during the FIFA World Cup in Germany in 2006, raumtaktik, run by Friedrich von Borries and Matthias Böttger, presented the Fanshop of Globalization in a 40ft container redesigned as a mobile fashion store. Funded by the German Federal Agency for Civic Education, it was stationed in various Germany cities on a weekly basis. Twenty-five outfits created by young German designers were presented in the store. Each outfit was made out of soccer jerseys, representing different teams and different aspects of globalisation. With 25 tales from the world of soccer, this project sheds light on the economic mechanisms, political circumstances and cultural contexts behind the changes taking place in the world economy today.

MMW ARCHITECTS OF NORWAY

FHILTEX
Norway, 1995

OPTREKTRANSVAAL
Tatsurou Bashi, KEEN

MOONRIDER
The Hague, Netherlands, 2005

The work of the Dutch artists' organisation OpTrek focuses on ongoing transformations in the Transvaal district of the Dutch capital the Hague. Three thousand public-sector rental housing units were due to be demolished here by 2004 and replaced with only 1,600 new dwellings – the majority of which are owner-occupied properties. Through a diverse programme of international art projects and activities, OpTrek is delivering a running commentary on the extensive urban development transformations in Transvaal.

PORTABLE CONSTRUCTION TRAINING CENTER
Los Angeles, USA, 1998

LOT–EK

MOBILE DWELLING UNIT
New York, USA, 2002

DOMESTIC SHED
New Orleans, USA, 2005

URBAN SPACE MANAGEMENT LTD.

COVE PARK ARTS CENTRE
Peaton Hill, Scotland, 2006

DE MARIA DESIGN ASSOCIATES INC.
Peter DeMaria with Christian Kienapfel

<u>REDONDO BEACH HOUSE</u>
Redondo Beach, USA, 2007

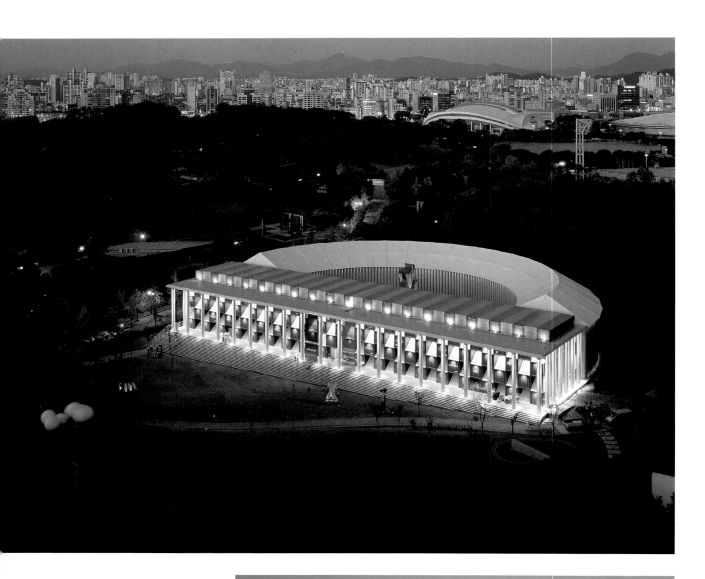

URBAN SPACE MANAGEMENT LTD.

CONTAINER CITY
London, United Kingdom, 2002

DE VIJF B.V. / SPACEBOX
Mart de Jong

<u>SPACEBOX</u>
Utrecht, Netherlands, 2004

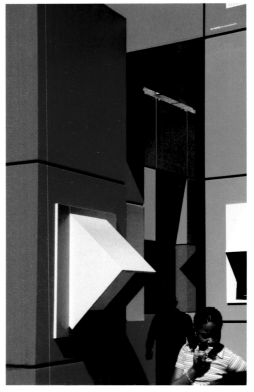

MAURER UNITED ARCHITECTS [MUA]

URBAN TETRIS
Amsterdam, Netherlands, 2001

Maastricht-based Maurer United Architects developed an exhibition system to showcase 25 artists' presentations on offbeat views of future living. The architects chose to transform the simple forms of the familiar first-generation computer game Tetris into three-dimensional exhibition stands. These stands were moved about over a period of several days throughout the city of Amsterdam and were then finally assembled as a pavilion reminiscent of the universally familiar Rubik's Cube.

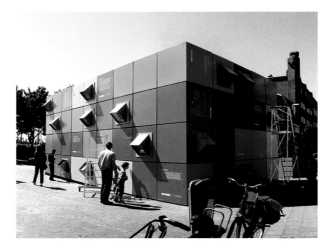

SHE_ARCHITEKTEN

ARCHITEKTURBOX
Hamburg, Germany, 2006

ATELIER KEMPE THILL

LIGHT BUILDING TRAVELLING MUSEUM PAVILION
Rotterdam, Netherlands, 2001

WOLFGANG WINTER AND
BERTHOLD HOERBELT

1 | **CASTLEFORD BELVEDERE**
Castleford, United Kingdom, 2006
2 | **9600: ZEEBRUGGE TRANSIT**
Zeebrugge, Belgium, 2003

KUBIK BERLIN
Berlin, Germany, 2006

Dozens of conventional 1,000-litre water tanks were used by the German architecture and art collective Modulorbeat to create a temporary light installation and club space on an abandoned lot near the river Spree in Berlin. The intention was to design an installation that provides both a room with an architectural structure and also a programmable lighting structure.

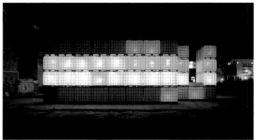

NARCHITECTS

UNPACKING
New York, USA, 2006

Unpacking by New York–based nARCHITECTS was a public installation commissioned by an automobile company for the New York launch of a new model. Designed to build up anticipation and create suspense, Unpacking slowly transformed over four days to finally reveal a void of the new model – as if the car had been subtracted from a block of ice, and then sliced into CT scans or sections.

NARCHITECTS

UNPACKING
New York, USA, 2006

PPAG ARCHITECTS
Anna Popelka, Georg Poduschka

YARD FURNITURE MUSEUMSQUARTIER
Vienna, Austria, 2003 – 2005

STADTMÖBEL
Hamburg, Germany, 2003

JENSKE DIJKHUIS

DREAM OF A CLOSET
Amsterdam, Netherlands, 2006

MATIAS CREIMER

<u>**PASADENA CITY COLLEGE PROJECT**</u>
Pasadena, USA, 2004

L.A.-based architect Matias Creimer supervised this student project at Pasadena City College in California. Together he and his students designed and constructed wooden structures that can be arranged in a line and read as one larger entity. Gaps and joints between segments had to be resolved by neighbouring teams to ensure a smooth formal transition. Although the nine structures are arranged in line, they can also form a circle, in that the first and last segments can also connect to each other.

**PARSONS THE NEW SCHOOL FOR DESIGN /
ST. ETIENNE SCHOOL OF ART AND DESIGN /
KONSTFACK UNIVERSITY OF COLLEGE OF
ARTS, CRAFT AND DESIGN**

LITTLE HOUSES ON THE BLACK RIVER
Hällefors, Sweden, 2006

In need of temporary housing for visiting
designers, Formen Hus, a museum and education centre in Hällefors, Sweden partnered
with Parsons The New School for Design,
St. Etienne School of Art and Design and
Konstfack University College of Arts, Craft
and Design to develop seasonal dwellings on
a former industrial railway bridge over the
Black River.

Taking inspiration from the traditional Swedish
cabin or friggebod, the dwellings are designed
as a kit of parts with built-in and modular furnishings that residents can configure to their
own liking. Constructed on moveable tracks,
the Little Houses feature two sleeping / living
compartments, a kitchen / bath compartment,
which also serves as a docking station during
the winter months, and a kit of provisions to
enhance the dwellings.

The M-House by American designer and artist Michael Jantzen is made from his M-vironment system, which features a wide variety of flexible components that can be connected in many different ways to a matrix of a modular support frames. The frames can be assembled and disassembled in different ways to accommodate a wide range of changing needs. The building consists of a series of rectangular panels that are attached with hinges to an open-space frame grid of seven interlocking cubes. The panels are hinged to the cubes either horizontally or vertically. The hinges allow the panels to fold into or out of the cube frames and perform various functions.

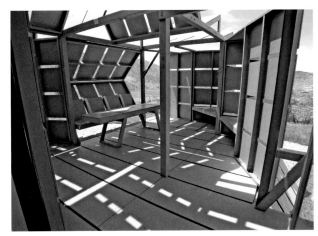

KORTEKINE STUHLMACHER ARCHITEKTEN

OVER THE TOP

BAUBOTANIK

LEONARD VAN MUNSTER

This section is dedicated to surprising add-ons to existing building structures and a variety of, often ironic, vertical extensions in city and rural areas. New living and working spaces are to be found here, from urban rooftop developments to tree houses located far away from civilisation.

Whilst the private enclave Lang/Baumann's Hotel Everland residing above the city rooftops exudes an air of gentrified jet-set zeitgeist, Stefan Eberstadt's Rucksackhaus, Santi Cirugeda's Puzzle-House or Frank Haverman's atelier extension generate parasitic additional spaces that dock onto existing buildings and benefit from their infrastructures. Temporary roof extensions such as Armand Gruentuch and Almut Ernst's Convertible City and Patrick Bouchain and Exyzt's Metavilla in the state pavilions in the Bienniale Giardini in Venice are further unconventional examples of vertical space extension. Many of the works presented here reside somewhere between art and architecture and illustrate creative perspectives on a cityscape that opens upwards. Erwin Wurm's House Attack, for example, crashes an entire family home into the roof of the Museum of Modern Art in Vienna and turns bourgeois preconceptions of house and home on their heads. Dadara's Love, Peace and Terror Tank stands guard above the rooftops of Amsterdam and in its ironic play on the visual language of war represents a symbol of peace. These and many more illustrate stimulating variations in approach to existing urban situations.

Whereas the first half of the works in this chapter are explicitly situated in an urban context, all the rest retreat back to nature and up into the trees. The palette of tree houses here ranges from David Greenberg's elementary hostels in the Nanshan Buddhist Culture Zone, Free Spirit Spheres Inc.'s suspended spherical domiciles and the technically demanding constructions from Baumraum to Terunobu Fujimori's one-man teahouses balanced on spindly wooden trunks and the overgrown architecture of Eduard Francois's Sproutling Building. This last project also bridges the gap to green asylums such as the wooden shingled, witches' hut-like Dragspelhuset by 24H Architecture, which, although it is not located up amongst the branches, still echoes that arboreal feeling.

All these raised retreats give flight to both fantasy and curiosity. In their apparent conquering of gravity, the lofty refuges awaken childhood memories and one's desire to climb a ladder once again up towards the sky and leave the banality of the everyday behind. Yet in contrast to glamorous penthouse apartments – the ultimate in luxury real estate - located both at the very top of the property ladder and city buildings, these featured projects inspire visions of a certain dreamy detachment. They are, in short, architectural expressions of the distinct will to remain aloof from conventional spatial modes of living and working: both literally and symbolically they have gone 'over the top'.

LANG / BAUMANN
Sabina Lang & Daniel Baumann

<u>HOTEL EVERLAND</u>
Leipzig, Germany, 2006–2007
Yverdon, Switzerland, 2002

This mobile, one-room hotel was created in 2002 by the Swiss artist duo L/B (Sabina Lang and Daniel Baumann) as an art project for the Swiss Expo02. The hotel was greeted by a storm of interest and would-be guests when it was first presented at Yverdon on Lake Neuchâtel. From June 2006 until August 2007 Hotel Everland was placed on the roof of the Leipzig Museum of Contemporary Art in Germany. In September 2007 Hotel Everland moved on to Paris, where it remained on the roof of Palais de Tokyo for one year.

KORTEKNIE STUHLMACHER ARCHITECTEN　　　**PARASITE LAS PALMAS**
Rotterdam, Netherlands, 2001

LOT—EK

GUZMAN PENTHOUSE
New York, USA, 1996

STEFAN EBERSTADT

<u>**RUCKSACK HOUSE**</u>
Cologne, Germany, 2005

Poised between art and architecture, form and function, private and public property, the Rucksack House is a hovering, illuminated space that looks like a cross between temporary scaffolding and minimal sculpture. 9 sq.m in size, the walk-in box is constructed from a welded-steel cage clad in exterior-grade plywood with an absorbent resin surface and punctuated by plexiglass inserts. The box is suspended from steel cables that are anchored to the roof or the façade of an existing building. Inside, light birch-veneered plywood covers all living surfaces. Fold-down furnishings and a multitude of built-in openings provide living space with access to direct daylight. Sections of the walls unfold, with the help of hidden magnets, into a desk, shelves, and a platform for reading or sleeping. Electricity is tapped from the 'host' house. As mobile as a rucksack, this mini-abode is intended as extra living space that can be taken along when the owners decide to move to a new home. The cube is light and open, free of connotations and adaptable to its users' needs.

PEANUTZ ARCHITEKTEN
Elke Knöß, Wolfgang Grillitsch

MÄRKISCHE HÜTTE
Berlin, Germany, 2005

Berlin-based Peanutz Architekten like to create laboratory conditions in the built environment in which to test various spaces of action. Here they set up a mountain cabin from which they served alpine delicacies on top of a high-rise social housing complex in Berlin's Märkisches Viertel – a suburban district of Berlin situated near the former border between West Berlin and East Germany.

INTACT
London, United Kingdom, 2004–2005

In a one-day illegal makeover a defunct
signal box on stilts in the London district of
Shoreditch was refurbished in a way that
aimed to express the idealised vision of a
dream property.
"Through a simple low-budget and temporary
action on a specific site, such projects capture
the imagination and raise awareness and
debate around spaces that we often pass by
without so much as a glance."

INTACT
London, United Kingdom, 2004–2005

ERWIN WURM

HOUSE ATTACK
Vienna, Austria, 2006

TAZRO NISCINO

ENGEL
Basel, Switzerland, 2002

For this 2002 project the Japanese artist Tazro Niscino encased the figure of an angel on top of the cathedral in Basle, Switzerland by building a room around it that was accessible to the public. The room consisted of walls and a ceiling supported by scaffolding. In this construction the artist seeks out various possible combinations for a variety of spheres: the intimate sphere of the living room together with the public nature of the location plus the public function of the religious sculpture combine to produce an alienating effect.

TAZRO NISCINO

ENGEL
Basel, Switzerland, 2002

GIANCARLO NORESE

ENGEL
Basel, Switzerland, 2002

PRECARIOUS HOME
Passo San Marco, Italy, 2007

JAN DE COCK

DENKMAL 2
Pasajes, Spain, 2004

The Belgian artist Jan de Cock is known for crossing the boundaries of the spaces assigned to him. For Manifesta 5, the European biennial of contemporary art, de Cock took over a shipbuilding warehouse that is a symbolic site in the Spanish port city of Pasajes. Here he sculpted alternative temporary constructions into the building itself. Working without plans, he obscured basic architectural features by developing an intricate construction over a period of two months that also transgressed conventional readings of interior/exterior and above/below. Denkmal 2 reassesses an interim architecture that resists strategies of design, practicality and function in order to develop an aesthetic system responding directly to context and the future possibilities of the site.

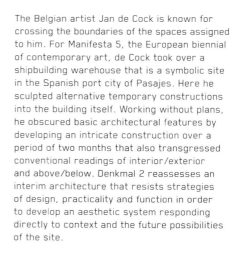

FRANK HAVERMANS

KAPKAR / TAW–BW–5860
Vught, Netherlands, 2004

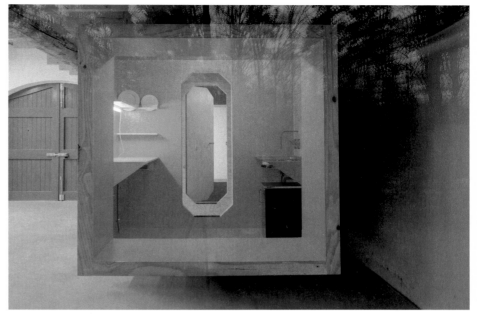

OPTREKTRANSVAAL
Michiel Voet, Jeroen Bisscheroux

JACK
The Hague, Netherlands, 2005

OPTREKTRANSVAAL
2012 Architecten

DAKLICHTERKER
The Hague, Netherlands, 2003

RECETAS URBANAS
Santiago Cirugeda

PUZZLE HOUSE
Seville, Spain, 2002

The Puzzle House by Santiago Cirugeda's Recetas Urbanas is a prototype for the creative occupation of empty lots within the old city of Seville in Spain. The temporary building was implemented without a developer by simply renting the land from its owner for an agreed minimal time period of four months. The structure housed cultural debates, political and tenant's meetings, and, of course, many drinking parties and urban barbecues that were well attended by friends and acquaintances.

GRÜNTUCH ERNST ARCHITEKTEN
Armand Grüntuch, Almut Ernst

EXYZT
EXYZT for Patrick Bouchain

METAVILLA
French Pavilion, La Biennale di Venezia,
Venice, Italy, 2006

ANDY HOLDEN

BLACK BOULDER MONOCHROME FOLLY
London, United Kingdom, 2006

The Black Boulder Monochrome Folly by British artist Andy Holden was set up as part of a self-organised event for a temporary public sculpture in Bedfordshire, England.

ANDY HOLDEN

GUSTON'S BOULDER
London, United Kingdom, 2004

DADARA

LOVE, PEACE AND TERROR TANK
Amsterdam, Netherlands, 2007

The prefabricated, four-barrelled, pink Love, Peace and Terror Tank by Amsterdam-based artist Dadara was set up on a rooftop in the centre of Amsterdam, keeping watch over the city.

"In the sixties, naked hippies with flowers braided into their long hair might have been successful in protesting against war, but nowadays the language of war itself might be a better vehicle for delivering a message of peace," says Dadara.

MICHAEL SAILSTORFER

HB-DAA
Germany, 2007

RECETAS URBANAS
Santiago Cirugeda

INSTITUTIONAL PROTHESIS
Castello, Spain, 2005

EDOUARD FRANCOIS

<u>SPROUTLING BUILDING</u>
Montpellier, France, 2000

BAUBOTANIK

Baubotanik, initiated by the German architects Ferdinand Ludwig, Oliver Storz and Hannes Schwertfeger, describes the idea of constructing load-bearing systems with living plants. The load-bearing system of the Living Skywalk is made from fast-growing willows, which support a platform that you can walk on. To highlight the contrast between the different characteristics of technical material on the one hand and living material on the other, the design contrasts living plant structures with a rigid geometry. The building is based on a growing root foundation and changes its shape over the seasons and years: in summer, leaves dominate the appearance, while in winter the strict structural form of trunks and steel is revealed. The skywalk is evolving its own character, shaped by its growing process, and therefore one can refer to a possible co-design with nature or a co-production between man and tree. Viewed from the position of architectural and cultural theory, Baubotanik presents a new relationship between nature and artefact within the discipline of architecture.

LEONARD VAN MUNSTER

<u>**UNDER HEAVEN** [1]</u>
Amsterdam, the Netherlands, 2004

For an exhibition at the Stedelijk Museum in Amsterdam, Dutch artist Leonard van Munster placed a tree (complete with tree house) on top of the 50-meter-high building. The tree house was made out of fruit crates and other found materials.

BAUMRAUM
Andreas Wenning

PEAR–TREE HOUSE
Heilbron, Germany, 2005

BAUMRAUM
Andreas Wenning

1 | **TREE HOUSE 'EILENRIEDE'**
  Hanover, Germany, 2006
2 | **TREE HOUSE BETWEEN ALDER AND OAK**
  Osnabrück, Germany, 2006

ATELIER BOW-WOW

MONKEY WAY
São Paolo, Brazil, 2006

For the São Paolo Biennial 2006 the Tokyo-based architecture office Atelier Bow Wow devised a bridge made of logs. Their so-called Monkey Way extended from the second-floor exhibition room of Oscar Niemeyer's Biennial Hall to some acacia trees adjacent to the building.

DAVID GREENBERG

NANSHAN BUDDHIST CULTURE ZONE
Hainan Island, China, 2006

ISLAND AMBIANCE
Jo Scheer

THE HOOCH
1 | Rincon, Puerto Rico, 2004
2 | Ashland, Oregon, 2005
3 | Venice Beach, California, 2006

KAPKAR / ZZW−220
Westkapelle, Netherlands, 2006

FREE SPIRIT SPHERES
Tom Chudleigh

page 112 / 113 | **TREE SPHERE**
British Colulmbia, Canada, 2007

The Dragspelhuset, by Rotterdam-based 24H Architecture, is an extension of a 19th-century cabin located on the shores of lake Övre Gla in the Glaskogen nature reserve in Sweden. 24H created an extension to the cabin that is capable of evolving. The building can literally adjust itself to its environment depending on weather conditions, season or the number of occupants. The extension is like a butterfly. During the winter it's a cocoon — compact with a double skin against the cold. During the summer the building can change its form or 'unfurl its wings' for extra shelter on rainy days.

SHANTY TOWN

SHOP ARCHITECTS

QUINZE AND MILAN

The dwellings here are inspired by informal building and settlement formats common to much of the developing world: so-called shanty towns. These projects combine the dynamic eclecticism of their subversive design mandate beyond standard blueprint mechanisms. Shanty Town covers variations of ancient hut-like buildings, garden sheds and green areas beyond the partitioned thinking of allotment culture, as well as socially engaged architecture projects that make use of salvaged materials to define their own language of form. Here too are three-dimensional space collages made from paper, cardboard and wood that reflect a whole new feeling for materiality.

A hut stands abandoned in a meadow, and in its simplicity and formal reduction to four plain walls and a pitched roof, reminds one of houses drawn by children. It is only when you get closer that the seams and breaks in Michael Sailstorfer's Heimatlied become irritatingly visible. Nathan Coley places Potemkin-like set buildings like decals in a variety of surroundings and thereby reveals the vacuity of domesticated bourgeois life. Simon Starling transports his bog-standard Shedhouse from the countryside into the white cube space of international galleries and the Hexenkessel und Strand GmbH moves a rural Thoreau-like log cabin into the city to serve as a temporary fairytale location. These and many of the other works shown here put simple refuges into the limelight which, in their lack of decoration, are reminiscent of the prototypical primitive hut.

The many-layered creations of Folke Köbberling and Martin Kaltwasser, often erected overnight using the simplest of materials and tools according to the motto 'one man's trash is another man's treasure,' take advantage of existing residual urban materials. The Madhousers' shelters for the homeless, the kindergarten buildings built by Volker Giencke and students at the University of Innsbruck, or even Akira Suzuki's Selfbuilt Shelters made of newspaper parcels, are all, beyond their idiosyncratic architectural language, of decisive importance in terms of the ethical demands of this form of design. Architecture is not an aesthetic end in itself, but a vehicle with which to help the socially disadvantaged get a roof over their heads. Suzuki's works in particular create a connection to a range of buildings that deal with the tectonic possibilities of recyclable materials such as paper and cardboard. Thus Rob Voerman develops accessible sculptures out of packing cases, RO&AD architecture covers the entire interior of an office with honeycomb cardboard, and with their curatorial work Cut for Purpose, Stealth Unlimited build a cardboard framework within an exhibition space, inviting artists to carve their own individual spaces out of it. The creative potential of wood structures is also sounded out in this chapter: Hitoshi Abe's wooden palettes twist up to the ceiling in his installations and the dizzying timber constructions from Interbreeding Field and Arne Quinze bridge both trade fair spaces and whole city streets.

By looking above and beyond the accepted material limits of house building, the constructions in this chapter demonstrate ingenious solutions and design strategies which, in their attempts to reuse what is available, connect to informal building and settlement formats and in their transformation of banal, everyday materials create aesthetically challenging spaces.

DIONISIO GONZÁLES

119

HEXENKESSEL & STRAND GMBH

MÄRCHENHÜTTE
1 | Berlin, Germany, 2006 / 2007
2 | Chelm, Poland, 2006

In the winter of 2006 / 2007 the Berlin-based Hexenkessel und Strand GmbH transposed an entire log cabin from eastern Poland to the city centre of Berlin to serve as a temporary stage for fairytale play performances for children.

NATHAN COLEY

SHOW HOME
United Kingdom, 2004

The Show Home is a temporary public art project by British artist Nathan Coley, curated by Locus+ and commissioned by North Tyneside Council. In this project the artist looks at the nature of the dream home as a concept that modern building developers sell as a lifestyle package. Coley brings a modest rural cottage into changing environments overnight and implements a promotional media campaign that large-scale builders employ to sell their new housing developments, to go with it.

121

MICHAEL SAILSTORFER

<u>HEIMATLIED</u>
Germany, 2001

For this project the German artist Michael Sailstorfer disassembled four automobile campers to construct a single house. Equipped with water and electricity, the fully functional building is located in a hilly landscape surrounded by fields and scattered houses.

WEXLER STUDIO
Allan Wexler

THE VINYL MILFORD
New York, USA, 1994

MICHAEL SAILSTORFER

<u>**WOHNEN MIT VERKEHRSANBINDUNG**</u>
Unter-/Oberkorb, Großkatzbach,
Anzing-Wilnham, Urtlfing, Germany, 2001

With Wohnen mit Verkehrsanbindung the German artist Michael Sailstorfer intervenes in public spaces by fitting four bus shelters in Bavaria with so-called 'survival furniture'. In his minimalistic, yet ironic, optimisation of the bus shelters, he furnishes them with a small-scale kitchen, bed, table, chair, lighting and fully functioning toilet.

SIMON STARLING

SHEDBOATSHED
Basel, Switzerland, 2005

FRIEDRICH VON BORRIES,
TOBIAS NEUMANN

DAHEIM
Berlin, Germany, 2002

MIKE MEIRÉ

THE FARM PROJECT
Cologne, Germany, 2007

As a contribution to the Dornbracht Edges series, the Farm Project is part of an investigative group of projects at the interface of architecture, design and art. Here the designer, curator and German brand director for Dornbracht, Mike Meiré, has designed a barn-like space housing a kitchen as a 'stage for life' that includes live pigs, birds and fish in an emotive ensemble.

"The lively jumble of smells, ingredients and spices, of cutlery, dishes, pots and pans. The kitchen as a place of tolerance, where food and drink, kitchen utensils and recipes from all over the world coexist. A place of the most varied artistic, architectural and cultural encounters."

24H ARCHITECTURE

DRAGSPELHUSET'S GUEST HOUSE
Glaskogen, Sweden, 2004

BARNSTORMERS

MOTION BARN
Salem, USA, 2006

ROBBRECHT EN DAEM ARCHITECTEN
Robbrecht en Daem Architecten with
Herman Seghers

WOODLAND CABIN
Southern Flanders, Belgium, 2002

HÜTTEN & PALÄSTE ARCHITEKTEN
Nanni Grau, Frank Schönert

GARDEN SALOON
Stuttgart, Germany, 2006

MINILAUBE (MILA)
Berlin, Germany, 2006

FELD72
feld72 & nan

TORONTO BARBECUE
Vienna, Austria, 2002

Through the acquisition of sub-divided green spaces which had a certain suburban feel through the use of hedges, the forecourt of the Museumsquartier in Vienna, Austria was mutated into a heterogenous allotment structure.

"Finely sculpted hedges, English lawns and small divisions of plots designated for specific uses: feld72 & nan made use of the hitherto unused forecourt as a private allotment. Some of the seventeen garden plots were privatized and operated by us and our friends. The variations in use were not assigned but rather presented under the heading, Cultivating the Field. The interpretation was open to each 'settler'. Lazing in the sun, bathing one's feet in a wading pool, mowing the lawn, picnicking and any other activities that realize the dream of having your own garden were imaginable. For the duration of the action, two garden sheds were erected that served as a home base and were occupied day and night."

WEXLER STUDIO
Allan Wexler

GARDENING SUKKAH
Ridgefield, USA, 2000

Gardening Sukkah, part of a series of pieces by New York-based artist Allan Wexler, explores the Jewish holiday of Sukkot. A celebration of the exodus from Egypt, Sukkot also marks the autumn harvest as the final gathering of food before winter. It is thought to be the inspiration for the American feast of Thanksgiving. For seven days the Gardening Sukkah shelters the family as they gather for Sukkot meals. For the remaining 357 days it houses gardening tools – another kind of celebration of the earth's bounty. Thus Gardening Sukkah connects and contrasts the functions of dining with those of gardening. The floor joists extend from the shed, allowing it to be transported like a wheelbarrow, while the windows of the dining room permit the movers to see through the building. Kitchen utensils are stored side by side, drawing connections between the functional and sculptural forms of each tool: a pitchfork to loosen the soil that grows the food, a fork to eat the food during the celebration of its harvest. Gutters collect the rainwater that falls on the roof for later use in the garden.

FARM DESIGN
Guy Brown

SHED
Loughborough, United Kingdom, 2005

NILS HOLGER MOORMANN

WALDEN
Lake Constance, Germany, 2006

PARK(ING) PROJECT
San Francisco, USA, 2005

PARK(ing), by REBAR, an open-source interdisciplinary collaborative group of creators, designers and activists based in San Francisco, investigates the reprogramming of a typical unit of private vehicular space by leasing a metered parking spot for public recreational activity.

"We identified a site in an area of downtown San Francisco that is underserved by public outdoor space and located in an ideal, sunny spot between the hours of noon and 2 pm. There we installed a small, temporary public park that provided nature, seating and shade. Our goal was to transform a parking spot into a PARK(ing) space, thereby temporarily expanding the public realm and improving the quality of the urban human habitat – at least until the meter ran out."

GRUPPO A12

GREEN ROOM
Busan, South Korea, 2006

The Green Room project by the Italian architect and artist collective Gruppo A12 was built for the Busan Biennial of Contemporary Art in Korea. A temporary garden in the form of a small room was installed near the city's main river. Its artificial 'nature' in a heavily built environment is a reflection on the ecological development of the area. It functions as a landmark and forms a spatial structure that enables the viewers to construct their own narratives depending on their location and viewpoint.

LEONARD VAN MUNSTER

UNDER HEAVEN [2]
Amsterdam Bijlmer, Netherlands, 2004

Under a viaduct in De Bijlmer – an infamous neighbourhood in Amsterdam – van Munster created a mirage with palm trees, banana trees and a waterfall.

GELITIN

STEFAN
New York, USA, 2001

THOMAS BRATZKE

ZAST HOUSE
Tokyo, Japan, 2005

For the Zast House, Berlin-based artist Thomas Bratzke built a small, L-shaped wooden house around a tree in Tokyo's popular Shibuya Park. Despite its small size it was equipped with a sleeping area, a sitting-room and an entrance area, and had little windows randomly arranged on the façade.

Pens and markers were attached to a simple Z-A-S-T relief that was applied to the outer skin of the building. Passers-by were invited to scribble on the building's façade with the pens, which they did with enthusiasm. After only a few days, hundreds of small drawings and messages gave the house a distinctive face. The interior of the house was restricted to the private use of the artist.

FOLKE KÖBBERLING & MARTIN KALTWASSER

FLYING BUILDINGS
Munich, Germany, 2006

Since 2002 the German architects and artists Folke Köbberling and Martin Kaltwasser have been intervening in public spaces by setting up temporary pavilions, hut villages and even whole houses — often overnight — that are ingeniously created from leftover materials discovered on the street, on wasteland and in rubbish dumps.

HAUS KÖLN
Cologne, Germany, 2005

FOLKE KÖBBERLING & MARTIN KALTWASSER   <u>HAUSBAU</u>
Gropiusstadt–Berlin, Germany, 2004

FOLKE KÖBBERLING & MARTIN KALTWASSER   <u>MUSTERHAUS</u>
Berlin, Germany, 2005

PUBLIC ARCHITECTURE

SCRAPHOUSE
San Francisco, USA, 2005

ScrapHouse was a temporary demonstration home, built entirely of salvaged material – ranging from street signs and shower doors to fire hoses and phone books – on Civic Center Plaza adjacent to San Francisco City Hall in the U.S.. Over the course of just six weeks, a team of volunteers scoured Bay Area dumps and scrap yards for materials. A group of architects, landscape architects, lighting specialists and metal sculptors gave these materials new life and ScrapHouse its final shape.

INTERBREEDING FIELD

WEN–HSIAN CONTEMPORARY ART GALLERY
Tainan, Taiwan, 2003

KLAUS STATTMANN

FLUC_2
Vienna, Austria, 2006

In a central urban planning site and busy traffic junction at Vienna's Praterstern, a pedestrian underpass and a former public restroom were transformed by Austrian architect Klaus Stattmann into the event club Fluc_2.

./STUDIO3 – INSTITUTE FOR EXPERIMENTAL ARCHITECTURE

OLIFANTSVLEI
Johannesburg, South Africa, 2006

Under the direction of Volker Giencke, the Institute for Experimental Architecture at the University of Innsbruck has been involved in various support projects for developing countries. For this low-tech and low-cost architecture project a group of students developed and built a kindergarten for the Olivantsvlei Primary School in Johannesburg, South Africa in collaboration with local workers within a period of six weeks.

147

MARJETICA POTRČ

HYRID HOUSE: CARACAS, WEST BANK, WEST PALM BEACH
USA, 2003

The work of this Slovenian artist deals with the gaps in knowledge that result when urban planners and architects insist on creating order. Potrč is particularly interested in what architects and planners cannot predict. Issues such as shanty towns, outsider communities, and the role of imagination are united in Potrč's work with an architecture of immediate, personal response.

"Hybrid Houses juxtaposes structures from the temporary architecture of Caracas, the West Bank and West Palm Beach, Florida, and shows how they negotiate space among themselves. Each of the community-based structures formulates its own language, which, in all three cases, has much in common with archetypal (and not modernist) architecture. Emphasis is placed on private space, security, and energy and communication infrastructures."

ATELIER VAN LIESHOUT

FAVELA
Netherlands, 2003

After several visits to the favelas of São Paulo, Atelier van Lieshout developed the idea of establishing a working relationship with favela dwellers. Five façades with windows and doors were made for this purpose in typical Atelier van Lieshout style. The plan was to give the façades to the future inhabitants and let them finish building the houses on site themselves with locally available materials.

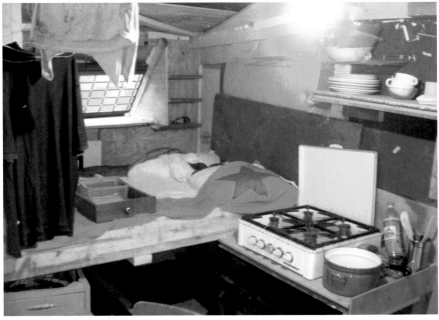

MARIA PADADIMITRIU

TEMPORARY AUTONOMOUS MUSEUM FOR ALL (T.A.M.A.)
Avliza / Athens, Greece, 1999

With her temporary and mobile architectural designs, Greek artist Maria Padadimitriu transformed a gypsy encampment on the outskirts of Athens into a Temporary Autonomous Museum for All (T.A.M.A.), where Vlach Romanian nomads collaborate with people from the art world and the general public.

DIONISIO GONZÁLEZ

1 | **JORNALISTA ROBERTO MARINHO II**
2004
2 | **SANTO AMARO III**
2006

ODA PROJESI

The Annex project by the Istanbul-based artists' collective Oda Projesi was featured in the Structure of Survival section of the 50th Venice Art Biennial in Italy. A prefabricated house designed for the survivors of an earthquake was moved from its original location in Adapazari, a Turkish region badly hit by the 1999 earthquakes, and transferred to Venice, where it served as a model and meeting point during the construction phase of the Biennial.

ULRIKE MYRZIK, MANFRED JARISCH

BLUE BOXES
Tokyo / Osaka, Japan, 2003

These pictures of homeless shelters in Tokyo and Osaka, Japan were taken by German photographers Ulrike Myrzik and Manfred Jarisch for an exhibition entitled Architecture of the Homeless at the Pinakothek der Moderne in Munich, Germany.

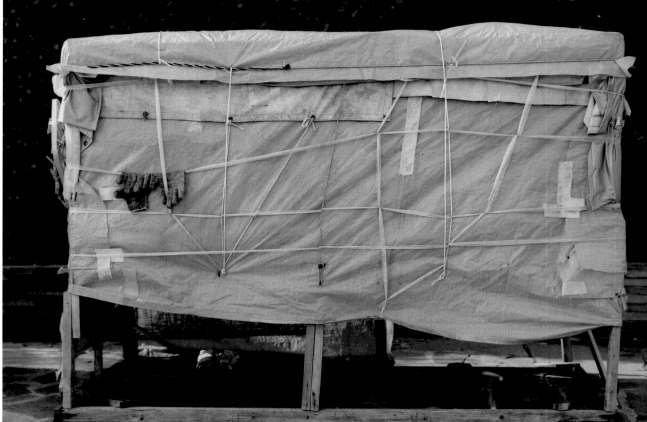

MAD HOUSERS

1 | **HOMELESS CAMP**
2 | **LOW RIDER**
3 | **LOCKING STORAGE UNIT**
4 | **THE HUT**
Atlanta, USA, 2004

The Mad Housers is a volunteer-run charitable organization in the U.S. dedicated to building free shelters for the homeless. Seeing the im-promptu cardboard and tarp shelters erected by homeless people in the city of Atlanta, they felt they could design structures that were safer and more secure. Aided by a network of helpers with pickup trucks and hammers, they were able to build and distribute small emergency shelters of their own design to Atlanta's homeless.

ATELIER BOW-WOW

PET ARCHITECTURE GUIDE BOOK EXHIBITION
Tokyo, Japan, 2000

The Japanese architects Atelier Bow Wow built a one-person model house in the MA gallery in Tokyo for the first exhibition of their Pet Architecture Guide Book. Due to limitations imposed by the gallery of one night for the construction of the exhibits and the small size of the elevator available for ferrying materials, Atelier Bow Wow decided to use small, light materials to build their structures made by bolting laminated rafters together. The placing of these rafters was varied to accommodate interior details such as furniture. The results were pieces of 'pet architecture' that was custom-designed, as opposed to emerging intrinsically from its surroundings.

ALEXANDER BRODSKY

VODKA CEREMONY PAVILION
Moscow, Russia, 2003

This project by Russian artist Alexander Brodsky was commissioned as an installation for the ArtKlyazma 2003 art festival in Moscow. It turned out to be an architectural statement through its use of material and cultural messages. It is a simple spatial and material metaphor of the Russian way of life. The building was partly inspired by Soviet resort architecture of the 1940s–50s. The main materials used are window frames salvaged from a demolition site in the centre of Moscow. These were fixed onto a simple wooden frame and painted white. Timber is used here as universal medium of architecture and memory. The 'ceremony' itself is quite simple: There is a basin of vodka on a table in the pavilion with two cups chained to the table. Visitors can drink vodka scooped from the basin with the cups.

ROB VOERMAN

REAL ESTATE
Berlin, Germany, 2006

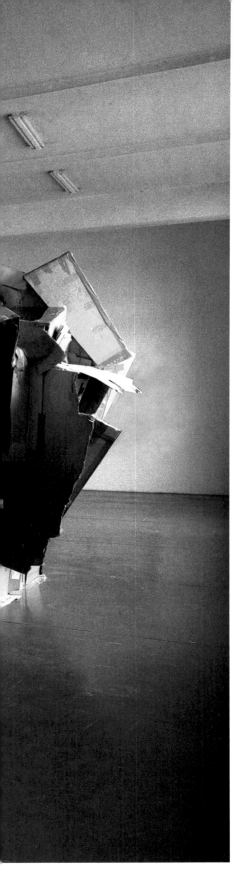

HYPERESPACE
St. Gallen, Switzerland, 2005

To celebrate the 20th anniversary of the Neue Kunst Halle in St. Gallen, Switzerland, the Geneva-based Chapuisat artist brothers created a 200 sq.m cardboard burrow in the main hall. As far as visitors were concerned, the only visible part of the project was the suspended entrance hole. Once plunged into darkness, they are then obliged to prostrate themselves and crawl into a tunnel, where they slide several metres towards the starting point of their adventure. Unable to turn back, they must then get on their knees and clamber, wriggle or squirm through the lair before emerging on the other side. Visitors are put to the test both physically and psychologically during their exploration, punctuated as it is by challenges of varying difficulty that push visitors to exceed themselves. The project invites social interaction, with initiated explorers attempting to dispel newcomers' fear of the unknown by convincing them of the simplicity of this pseudo-subterranean assault course.

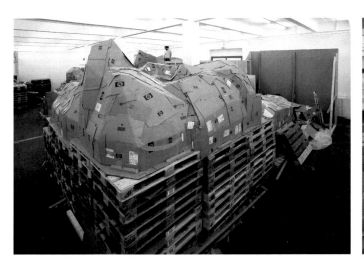

APRÈS–NOUS
Helga Blocksdorf, Florence Girod,
Catharina Förster

FITTING ROOM
New York, USA, 2007

Since 2000 the Berlin–based group Après–Nous has been working on temporary installations in empty shop spaces. With their recent performance Fitting Room, privately owned public space in New York City was transformed into a cultural living space. Leftover cardboard was gathered from the streets and then transformed into urban furniture in the showroom in Lower Manhattan as take–away objects for visitors. The boundaries between interior and urban space blur and the former found objects spill back into the city imbued with new meaning.

MATS KARLSSON

FASHION SHOW
Kortrijk, Belgium, 2006

RO&AD ARCHITECTEN

STEALTH.UNLIMITED
Ana Dzokic, Mario Campanella, Marc Neelen

CUT FOR PURPOSE
Rotterdam, Netherlands, 2006

For this project the Rotterdam-based architects STEALTH.unlimited were asked to challenge the role and potential of a new space to be initiated within the Museum Boijmans van Beuningen in Rotterdam, Netherlands. The resulting Cut for Purpose project was in place for over two months during 2006. It was based on a temporary inversion of the logic and use of given gallery space through a physical intervention and a transformative process set within it. To do so, an immense structure of honeycomb cardboard was installed to fill almost the entire space. The curators invited various individuals to initiate activities within the project. Each person participating in the experiment had to negotiate and physically carve out their own territory within the cardboard spatial structure. Thus spaces were purpose-cut for specific events or given a new use through sharing, extending, squatting or other interventions.

Artists featured: Ernest van der Kwast, Stadsredactie, Wendelien van Oldenborgh, Strange Attractors, Cucosa artists collective, Robbert de Vrieze and many more

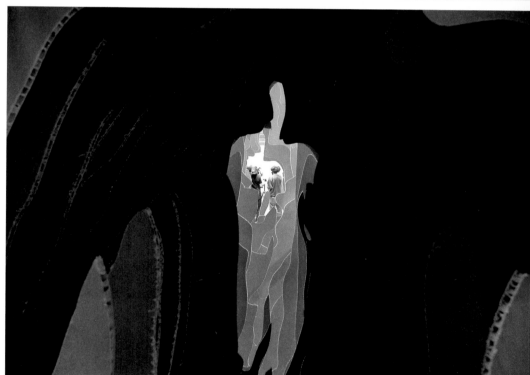

MARTTI KALLIALA AND ESA RUSKEEPÄÄ
WITH MARTIN LUKASCYZK

MAFOOMBEY
Helsinki, Finland, 2005

ATELIER HITOSHI ABE
Hitoshi Abe

<u>**PALLET**</u>
Miyagi Museum of Art, Sendai, Japan, 2003

DUNESCAPE AT P.S.1
New York, USA, 2000

The Museum of Modern Art and the P.S.1 Contemporary Art Center in New York jointly sponsor the MoMA / P.S.1 Young Architects Program, an annual series of competitions that gives emerging architects the opportunity to build projects conceived for P.S.1's facility in Long Island City. SHoP was selected to create the debut project in the series – a dunescape, known as Warm Up 2000, for summer relaxation in P.S.1's outdoor courtyard.

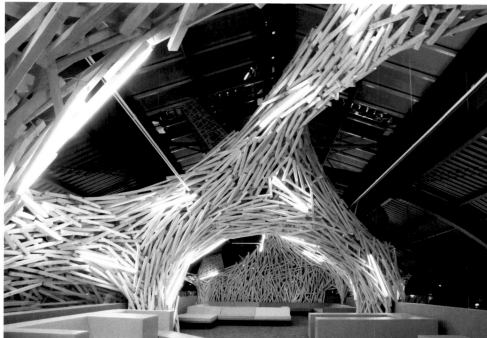

INTERBREEDING FIELD

NON SIDE ZOOM
Tainan, Taiwan, 2005

Interbreeding Field is an experimental architectural laboratory based in Tainan, Taiwan.
It was founded by its director Li H. Lu at the
Tainan National University of the Arts in 1999.
"The philosophy of Interbreeding Field is to
create new directions in architecture, conduct
experiments and reconstruct the matrix of
sensitive genes. The Interbreeding Field has
been engaged in compound construction,
production, breeding, creating and developing,
then atmosphere compounding."

UCHRONIA
Black Rock Desert, Nevada, USA, 2006

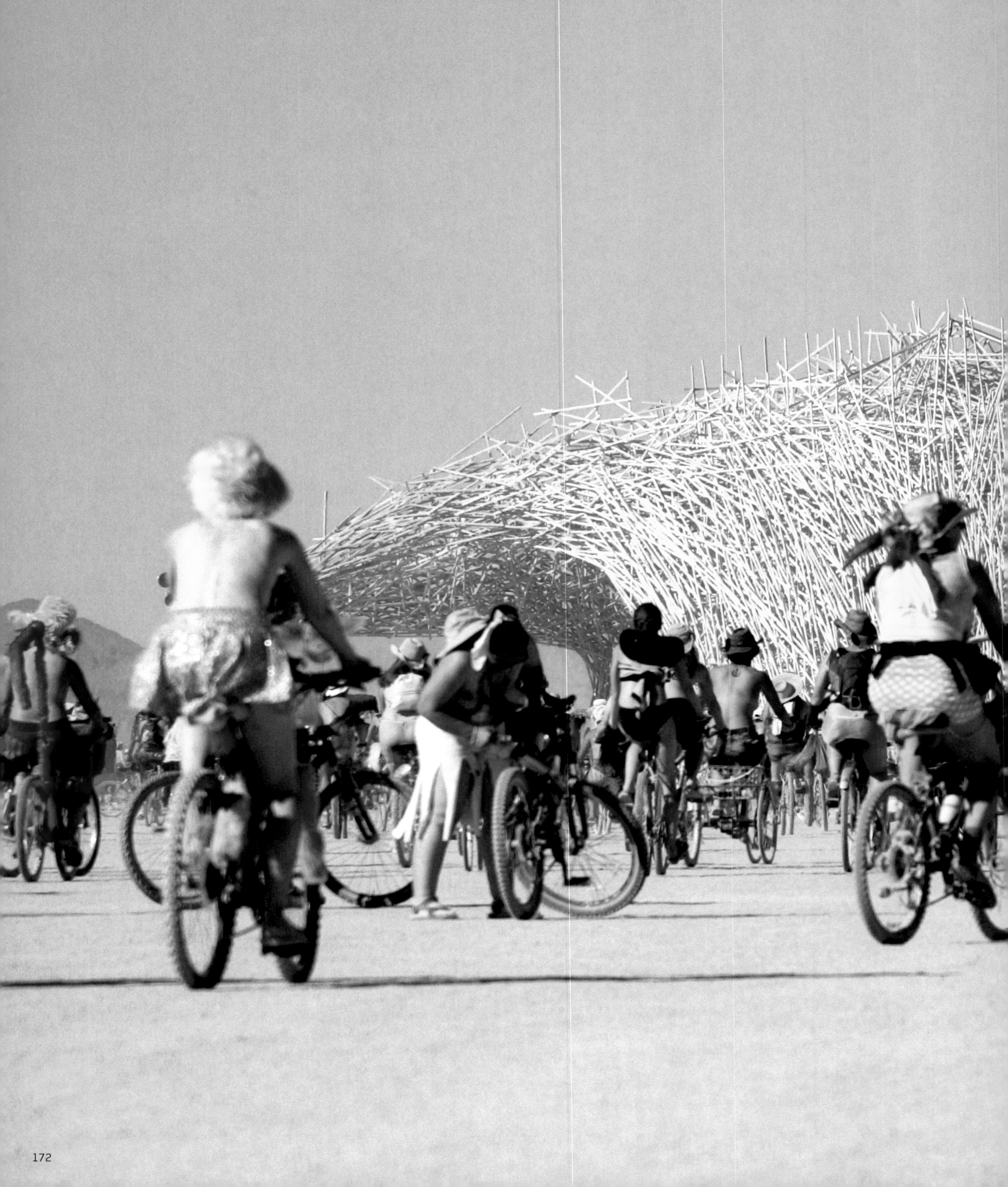

Bringing creative minds together and forging a strong sense of creative collaboration was the intention when Brussels-based designers Jan Kriekels and Arne Quinze directed 90 volunteers to build a unique installation made of wooden battens and nails as part of the annual Burning Man Festival in the Black Rock Desert, Nevada in 2006. At 200 x 100 x 50 ft, it was a gigantic but short-lived work of art since it was then promptly burned to the ground by its creators.

"This was in a way, a portal, showing us what the world could be like if creativity ruled supreme. Looking up at the installation, many saw how their future could be. Now, that future will become a reality."

UCHRONIA
Jan Kriekels and Arne Quinze

UCHRONIA
Black Rock Desert, Nevada, USA, 2006

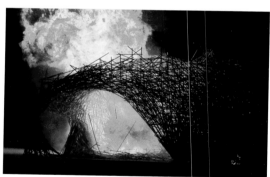

INTERBREEDING FIELD

TREE HOUSE 2 – DOWN TO THE ROOTS SERIES
Tainan, Taiwan, 2004

DO-HO SUH

SHOWTIME

This final chapter is dedicated to performative spaces in art and architecture. An intriguing collection of hybrids is to be found here whose emphasis lies on the theatrical impact of space. Thus it concerns the works of artists and architects who challenge and go beyond the bounds of their own disciplines, from purely artistic space interventions to media-inspired urban space performances as well as active participatory practices in alternative space occupation. To a certain extent the space-generating practices presented in previous chapters are here taken both to and beyond their artistic limits.

COLLEGE OF ENVIRONMENTAL DESIGN

A massive fake mountain towers over the Austrian pavilion at the Venice Art Biennale; an empty Prada shop stands abandoned by the road in the Texan desert like a mirage; an entire apartment is faithfully reproduced in 1:1 detail in transparent fabric and a breakneck rollercoaster is implanted in an exhibition space on the first floor of a gallery. These and many other examples are expressions of overstepping the boundaries of traditional concepts and presentation forms in contemporary art, like Thomas Demand and Olafur Eliasson's works that recall recently landed spaceships, or the fascinating Styrofoam miniature worlds of Tom Sachs' where model car race tracks snake through the room past various icons of modern architecture such as Le Corbusier's l'Unité de Habitation and Villa Savoye, as well as an urban ghetto scenario and a branch of McDonalds – all in 1/25th scale. In all of them, the movement towards space itself is palpable, but so too are expansions of urban space through the use of new media and technologies: the key word here is 'interaction'. Entire façades become screens for colourful illuminations, large-scale light tags are projected onto house walls and newspaper headlines are provocatively projected from a moving vehicle onto the passing cityscape.

A further group of projects makes use of the simplest of methods to interact with urban surfaces: Florentijn Hoffman highlights empty residential complexes by drenching them in monochrome colours so that they are visible from far and wide; Luis Berrios Negron paints the post-war city of Kabul with his huge, striking works, and the blinding white of François Roche's snake-like extension of an exhibition space drives the concept of the white cube at the point of complete disintegration to the extreme. But the intense superficiality of a clothing-covered building on the Campo Santa Margherita in Venice from Matej Andraž Vogrinčič, the imploding house by the Artist's League Houston and the ice-bound architectural poetry of the Snow Show also reflect an elementary awareness for the performative potential of the haptic and sensual qualities of architectural space.

New approaches are being formulated in the playful and spontaneous perception and use of urban space that increasingly highlight the dynamic, transversal and performative nature of architecture and city planning. In this way, temporary interventions in the extant cityscape – such as the complizen's Sportification, the Hier Entsteht Event in front of the Berlin Volksbühne theatre or the Babylonian heights of the towering sculpture by Peter Fattinger, Veronika Orso and Michael Rieper – transform it into an open laboratory whose experimental character spreads well beyond disciplinary boundaries.

This chapter forms the creative culmination of Spacecraft. The manifold practices related to architecture, city and space presented here, in their acts of transgressing conventional perceptions in architecture and art, unlock new fields of action and open up new horizons on the performance value of space.

FRANKA HÖRNSCHEMEYER

ANDREA ZITTEL

1 | **A–Z HOMESTEAD OFFICE FOR LISA IVORIAN–GRAY**
California, USA, 2003

2 | **A–Z HOMESTEAD UNIT FROM A–Z WEST WITH ROUGH FURNITURE**
California, USA, 2004

ROB VOERMAN

BAD HABITS
London, United Kingdom, 2004

<u>**THE EXCHANGE STUDENT**</u>
Oslo, Norway, 2006

This installation was originally created for an exhibition in a former studio building at the Academy of Arts in Oslo, Norway. Berlin-based artist Stefan Eichhorn installed a hidden, elevated room, approximately 80 cm away from the original walls, with a sleeping bunk, a bed and several shelves. A small door in the side wall and a ladder connected the new room with the exhibition space.

HANS SCHABUS

SHOULD I LEAVE OR SHOULD I GO
Milan, Italy, 2006

ERWIN WURM

FAT HOUSE
Basel, Switzerland, 2004

PRIMITIVO SUAREZ–WOLFE

OVERTURN
Los Angeles, USA, 2000

HANS SCHABUS

THE LAST LAND
Austrian Pavilion, La Biennale di Venzia,
Venice, Italy, 2005

For the 2005 Venice Art Biennial, Hans Schabus transformed the Austrian pavilion into an alpine fortress, with galleries leading to the summit and from darkness into the light. Confronting the viewer with a mountain-like barrier, the pavilion was massively present although its own architecture was scarcely visible. Here it is not the pavilion which imposes itself on the artwork but the artwork that imposes itself on the pavilion.

RICHARD WILSON

FACE LIFT
London, United Kingdom, 1991

STUDIO ROOSEGAARDE
Daan Roosegaarde

LIQUID 2.0
Rotterdam, Netherlands, 2006

Rotterdam-based Studio Roosegaarde explores and realises projects in art and technology. Based in the home of Daan Roosegaarde, it functions as a laboratory in which new alliances are formed with software engineers, material manufacturers and cultural foundations for each project.

This is an interactive living cocoon that physically adapts to sounds and motion generated by visitors: "The moment a visitor entered, Liquid 2.0 lifted up its roof to make more space for the new inhabitant. This resulted in an object which, although filled with new media, seems 'natural' for the visitor, as an extension of their skin. 'Natural', of course, in a 22nd-century way." Daan Roosegaarde

OLAFUR ELIASSON

LA SITUAZIONE ANTISPETTIVA
Kanazawa, Japan, 2003

This installation is formed from approximately 250 stainless steel polygonal cones whose inner surfaces are highly polished. From the outside, the triangulated rib structure, bolts, and untreated steel are exposed and viewers are offered only glimpses of the kaleidoscopic interior through the truncated ends of the cones.

The elevated ellipsoidal space is entered via a short flight of stairs. Once inside, the viewer stands on an open metal-grill floor that affords a 360-degree view of the space. Here he/she is confronted with a seemingly infinitely faceted space with multiple fragmented reflections of him/herself and other visitors. The endlessly mirrored, kaleidoscopic interior is thus in stark contrast to the rough exterior. Light is emitted via the cut ends of the hexagonal cones and the narrow doorways.

La Situazione Antispettiva was originally installed as a walk-through space that constituted part of a sequence of installations in and around the Danish pavilion at the 50th Venice Biennale, 2003. The artwork was later reinstalled at the 21st Century Museum of Contemporary Art, Kanazawa, Japan, in 2004, where it was modified to have only one entrance/exit.

THOMAS DEMAND

<u>**SPACE SIMULATOR**</u>
Berlin, Germany, 2003

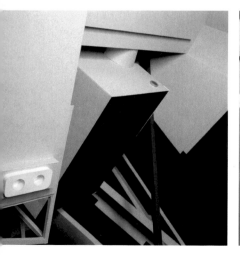

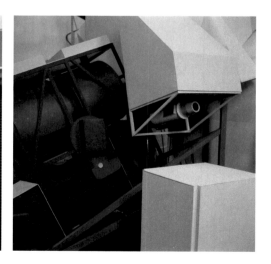

1 | **MEAT MARKET**
North Melbourne, Australia, 2004
2 | **ONE MORE THING**
New York, USA, 2005

SHAHRAM ENTEKHABI

PARASITE ARCHITECTURE
Cracow, Poland, 2006

ENCORE HEUREUX
Nicola Delon, Julien Choppin

HERBES FOLLES
Paris, France, 2003

OSA OFFICE FOR SUBVERSIVE ARCHITECTURE

<u>**KUNSTHÜLLE**</u>
Liverpool, United Kingdom, 2006

The Kunsthülle is a temporary installation for the Greenland Street Arts Centre – a major new venue for contemporary art in Liverpool. The rooftop structure is a playful and experimental space for lectures, performances and events. It appears to merge into the old factory building, incorporating an existing staircase and the rooftop, and extending out over the public façade. The installation consists of a pavilion structure that divides the rooftop into two terraced spaces lined with green hedges. A permeable membrane, or flexible curtain, allows visitors to pass from one space to another.

NONCON:FORM
Gruber Leitner Nageler Ohrhallinger OG

TEMPORARY OUTDOOR AUDITORIUM
Haag, Austria, 2000

JESKO FEZER / MATHIAS HEYDEN

<u>HIER ENSTEHT (STRATEGIES OF
PARTICIPATIVE ARCHITECTURE AND
SPATIAL APPROPRIATION)</u>
Berlin, Germany, 2003

Hier Entsteht was a 14-day building experiment, an exhibition, a lecture series and an open space for spontaneous settlements and unpredictable activities. It took place on a 200 sq.m platform that was erected in Berlin, Germany above a small pavilion hosting an exhibition on participative architecture from the 1960s to the late 1980s. The large rooftop provided space for daily lectures, presentations, cooking, a bar, music performances and diverse gatherings and discussions. Here, at four metres above ground level, a new layer of urban space was created, unfettered by building regulations. The project team used found materials to develop and create a small social system containing two bars, a music pavilion, an herb garden, a shower, some small exhibitions, a camping hotel and several barbecue sites. Hier Entsteht was part of the project ErsatzStadt (Ersatz City) in cooperation with the Volksbühne am Rosa-Luxemburg-Platz theatre and the Kulturstiftung des Bundes. It was developed, curated, designed and executed by a group of architecture students from the Universität der Künste (University of the Arts) in Berlin under the guidance of Jesko Fezer and Mathias Heyden.

BERT NEUMANN / LSD BERLIN

FRANK CASTORF'S DER IDIOT
Freie Volksbühne, Berlin, Germany, 2002

HAWORTH TOMPKINS

ALMEIDA AT GAINSBOROUGH STUDIOS
London, UK, 2001

Searching for a temporary venue in which to stage large-scale productions, the Almeida Theatre in London commissioned British architects Haworth Tompkins to convert a derelict power station in Shoreditch into a temporary theatre space at the lowest possible cost. The result was a spectacular yet surprisingly intimate stage and auditorium, where the old building was allowed to become an integral and essential part of the performances. Having played to full houses here for every performance throughout the summer of 2000, the theatre's temporary venue was closed at the end of the season and has now been demolished.

VAZIO S/A ARQUITETURA E URBANISMO
Carlos M Teixeira & Louise Marie Ganz

<u>TOPOGRAPHICAL AMNESIAS II</u>
Belo Horizonte, Brazil, 2004

The backdrop for this project by Vazio S/A (Void Inc.), a Brazilian collective of architects, engineers, landscape designers and artists, were buildings in a mountainous, middle-class district of Belo Horizonte in Brazil that were designed for hilly terrain but without any consideration of topography. This architecture resulted in the so-called concrete palafittes found under the buildings; an eerie, suburban cityscape of concrete pillars that are sometimes the same height or are even taller than the buildings they support.

Vazio S/A's Topographical Amnesias II project was an intervention commissioned by the street-theatre company Armatrux with the objective of triggering new uses for these voids. It was marked by a stage/auditorium made of suspended gardens, wooden platforms, ladders, ramps and a large biodegradable blanket that covered the backdrop of the palafittes. The sequence of contiguous pillars was penetrated by walkways threading between two buildings and winding up four floors above the access level, which was a vacant plot behind the palafittes.

**PETER FATTINGER, VERONIKA ORSO,
MICHAEL RIEPER**

ADD ON. 20 HÖHENMETER
Vienna, Austria, 2005

For six weeks the add on. 20 höhenmeter project by Vienna-based architects and designers Petter Fattinger, Veronika Orso and Michael Rieper transformed Vienna's Wallensteinplatz into a centre of urban interaction. A temporary sculpture capable of communicating and interacting with the general public was set up as an accessible object with its own infrastructure in the middle of an urban square. The basic structure of add on. consisted of different platforms up to a height of twenty metres. In them, custom-made spatial modules interlocked with prefabricated parts that had been imaginatively altered from their original functions. As an environment accessible to the general public, the installation's entire structure was an invitation to explore new worlds and offered a wide range of views and vistas from various levels. The result was a fascinating diversity of perspectives on everyday life, on our surroundings in general and, more specifically, on the location of the platform itself. Accommodation was available in a separate wing: guests could stay overnight in various modules designed by architecture students. Offering a dense programme of daily events, add on. also functioned as a venue for lectures, concerts, projects by visiting artists and film screenings.

COMPLIZEN PLANUNGSBÜRO
Tore Dobberstein, Andreas Haase

SPORTIFICATION
Halle Neustadt, Germany, 2003

The Sportification project by complizen Planungsbüro, a German office for architecture, communication and urban development, examines how much fun, sport and initiative is possible in existing urban structures and how much urbanity can be integrated into sports. Since 2002 complizen Planungsbüro has been using urban sports to activate city spaces. The project was initiated in eastern Germany, where countless buildings are empty and derelict. Many of them have already been demolished, many will be in the future. Sportification defines urban void areas as a competitive advantage and envisions an urban future where the entire city turns into a landscape of obstacles and playgrounds.

NUTSY'S
New York, USA, 2001–2002

A large, complex work covering approximately 4,000 sq.ft, Tom Sachs's Nutsy's is a world of sculptural, mechanical and video elements united by a roadway that traverses the entire installation. Nutsy's links the idealistic modernism of Le Corbusier with the commercialised modernism of McDonald's.

American artist Tom Sachs creates three-dimensional collages that include architectural models of icons of the modern age such as Le Corbusier's Unité d'Habitation and Villa Savoye, and also urban ghetto scenes including typical McDonald's branches. Built mostly with foam core, a hot glue gun and drawing pens, the models are on a 1:25 scale and nearly all are white. The Nutsy's installation also utilises scavenged street lumber, asphalt, a radar gun, alcohol, turntables and LPs. The entire installation is navigated by remote-control toy racing cars. These cars and their racetrack are the connective tissue that binds the disparate parts of Nutsy's world together, from the 'ghetto' and 'modernist art park' to the 'bong-hit station' and 'piss station.' Another ingredient of this world is a gigantic 10,000-watt boom box. Kiosks showing videos that represent the time-based aspects of the work are included in the installation as well.

FRANKA HÖRNSCHEMEYER

1 | **BFD – BÜNDIG FLUCHTEND DICHT**
Deutscher Bundestag, Berlin, Germany, 2001
2 | **BÜROAUFLÖSUNG**
Berlin, Germany, 2001

The main subject matter of German artist Franka Hörnschemeyer's work is space. By addressing the viewer's relationship with un-perceived aspects of space and by her unique method of utilising building materials, she con-fronts us with a new spatial experience that challenges our understanding of architecture. The artist's definition of space is not a tradi-tional one: matter and space are equal. The materials she uses, such as gyprock, form-work panels and plywood shuttering, originate from an architectural context and are re-used to produce new ensembles.

REALITIES:UNITED
Tim Edler and Jan Edler

MUSEUM X
Mönchengladbach, Germany, 2006

Museum X by the Berlin-based brothers and founders of realities:united, Tim and Jan Edler, was conceived as a temporary installation in Mönchengladbach to act as a surrogate and social bookmark for Hans Hollein's Abteiberg Museum while it was closed for renovation. The central motivation behind this project was to expand beyond the original mandate of 'sculpture as urban sign' into the realm of 'museum as sculpture'. Through the use of broad façade panels and other components the centrally located, large-scale structure, of the former Mönchengladbach theatre was transformed into an imaginary museum building designed in a distinctive post-war modernist style. This clearly discernable illusion of a cultural building, conceived as an 'urban status symbol', is detailed all the way through to the entrance foyer, which is staffed with ersatz museum personnel.

1

1 | The original building from 1959 by Paul Stohrer before the intervention by realities: united

MICHAEL ELMGREEN / INGAR DRAGSET

PRADA MARFA
Texas, USA, 2005

A sculpture by Berlin-based artists Michael Elmgreen and Ingar Dragset, Prada Marfa is located on a patch of desolate ranching land near Marfa, outside the town of Valentine, Texas on Highway 90. As one approaches the artwork by car, it appears to be a large minimalist sculpture. As one gets closer, it appears to be a luxury boutique where a display of high-heeled Prada shoes and bags from the fall 2005 collection can be seen through the shop windows. Yet one cannot open the door; it is a sealed time capsule and will never function as a place of commerce.

KREISSL KERBER
Alexa Kreissl, Daniel Kerber

<u>**PAVILION OF DRIFTING EXPECTATIONS**</u>
Berlin, Germany, 2004

With their work Pavilion of Drifting Expectations, the Berlin-based artists Alexa Kreissl and Daniel Kerber created a large styrofoam sculpture based on a small-scale model of an earthquake site in Turkey. A video shot during the destruction of the pavilion by the artists themselves was then presented as a life-size projection and became a sculptural installation in its own right.

ARNO BRANDLHUBER
b&k+ Arno Brandlhuber & Markus Emde
with Thomas Demand

**GERMAN CONTRIBUTION FOR THE
26TH BIENNIAL OF SÃO PAULO**
São Paulo, Brazil, 2004

German architect Arno Brandlhuber of the firm
b&k+ developed an exhibition concept for the
artist Thomas Demand at the biennial in São
Paulo. In the exhibition building, designed
by Oscar Niemeyer, the architect set up a
walk-in model of part of the building within the
building itself. The model, situated around the
escalator on the ground floor, was a precise
1:10 scale copy of a cinema space on the third
floor. As one enters this space, it seems at
once familiar and yet unsettling at the same
time. The subtle architectural mimicry at work
here induces an imperceptible psychological
disturbance for the viewer.

FLUX ROOM
New York, USA, 2002

The Flux Room by Reiser + Umemoto, RUR Architecture P.C. is a flexible space–modulation machine designed to register the changing effects of magnetic fields. The installation has been displayed internationally in various museum spaces. Suspended within this room are approximately 4,000 equally spaced magnetic needles loosely attached to tensioned nylon line so as to move freely in the X, Y and Z axes. The magnetic fields are generated by a series of solenoids located within the space. The solenoids are linked by a control system that can modulate the strength of the magnetic fields given off by the solenoid array to produce a range of rhythmic flows through the needles in the space. In general, the installation is a highly mobile one that can generate a wide range of field effects, for example schools of fish, wind on fields of grain, clouds, vortices etc.

ELECTROLAND LLC

ENTERACTIVE
Los Angeles, USA, 2006

L.A.-based Electroland is a team that creates large-scale public art projects and electronic installations. Each project is site-specific and may employ a broad range of media, including light, sound, images, motion, architecture and interactivity.

In this project at 11th and Flower Street in Los Angeles, a large interactive carpet of LED tiles located at a building entrance detects visitors and displays interactive light patterns in response. At the same time, a massive arrangement of LED light fixtures on the building face displays these responsive light patterns to the surrounding city. Visitors crossing the carpet can simultaneously see the effects of their actions beneath their feet and a view of them on the building façade via a video transmission from across the street.

**LAB(AU) I LABORATORY FOR
ARCHITECTURE AND URBANISM**

<u>TOUCH</u>
Brussels, Belgium, 2007

The Brussels-based design collaborative
Laboratory for Architecture and Urbanism
[Lab(au)] creates interactive artworks, audio-
visual performances and scenographies that
examine the transformation of architecture
and spatio-temporal structures. This particular
project centres around the 145m Dexia Tower in
Brussels. The tower's 4,200 windows can be
individually lit in colour, thus turning the building into an architecture of light. The lighting
pattern is based on the tower's architectural
and urban characteristics using parameters
such as its orientation, volume and scale.
From a specially designed pavilion at the bottom
of the tower, people can interact with the
light installation through a multi-touch screen
in real time, either individually or collectively.
Both static (touch) and dynamic input (gesture)
can be recognized by the installation's program
to generate an elementary graphical language
of points, lines and surfaces.

USMAN HAQUE (HAQUE DESIGN + RESEARCH)

OPEN BURBLE
Singapore, 2006

In Open Burble by London-based architect Usman Haque, members of the public came together to compose, assemble and control an immense rippling, glowing, bustling 'burble' that swayed in the evening sky in response to the crowd interacting below. The resulting massive structure existed at such a large scale that it was able to compete visually in an urban context with the skyscrapers that surround it.

The Burble was constructed from a set of 140 modular and configurable carbon-fibre units approximately 2m in diameter. Each unit was supported by seven extra-large helium balloons which contained sensors, LEDs and microcontrollers, enabling balloons and units to co-ordinate and create patterns of colour that rippled up towards the sky.

Part installation, part performance – for the design and assembly by the public was as much a part of the project as the actual flying – the Burble enabled people to contribute at an urban scale to a structure that occupied their city, albeit for only one night.

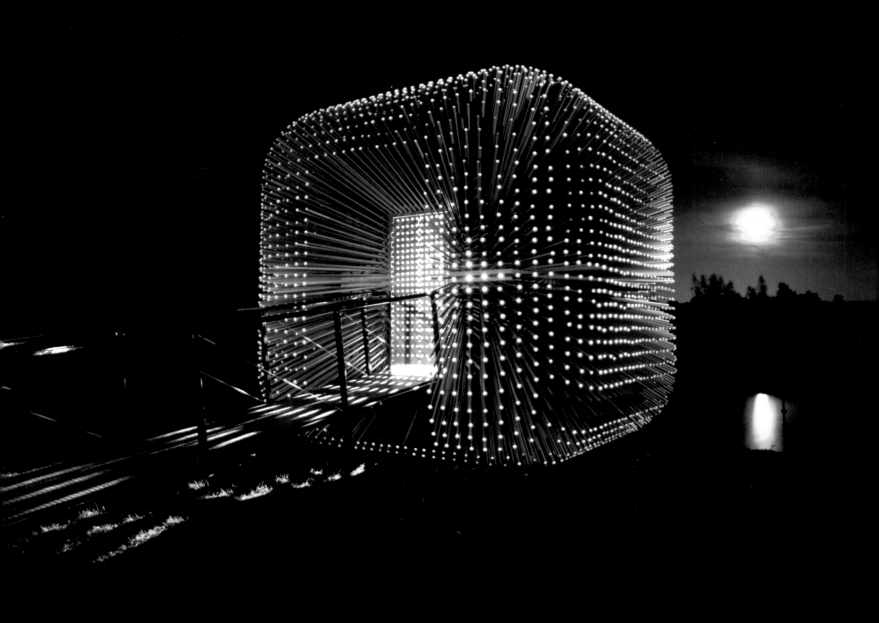

HEATHERWICK STUDIO

<u>SITOOERIE</u>
Barnard's Farm, United Kingdom, 2000

STUDIO ROOSEGAARDE
Daan Roosegaarde

DUNE 4.0
Amsterdam, Netherlands, 2006

This is an interactive landscape that reacts to the behaviour of people. As a hybrid of nature and technology, it comprises a large quantity of fibres that brighten in response to the sounds and motion of passing visitors. Dune 4.0 investigates nature in a futuristic relationship with urban space by means of looking, walking and interacting. Dune 4.0 is currently being developed further by Studio Roosegaarde for a public site in Rotterdam.

3DELUXE

CYBERHELVETIA PAVILION
Biel / Bienne, Switzerland, 2002

Taking its cue from traditional Swiss swimming pools, the Cyberhelvetia Pavilion at the Swiss Expo02 was conceived by the German design collective 3deluxe as a place of personal encounter and communication. A shiny blue glass block replaced the real swimming pool and visitors were invited to immerse themselves in the multilayered atmosphere of a virtually expanded reality.

The pool was filled with virtual water, which visitors could enhance by adding imaginary life forms both on site and via the internet. The interaction between real and virtually present people and digital creatures constantly created new atmospheric images on the projected surface of the pool, so that the overall impression was essentially that of a living organism. Various interactive games on the surface and along the sides of the pool offered guests the opportunity to make contact with other guests. Like nearby Lake Bienne, the artificial surface of the water changed during the course of the day and seasons, and thus linked the artificial with nature and the virtual with reality.

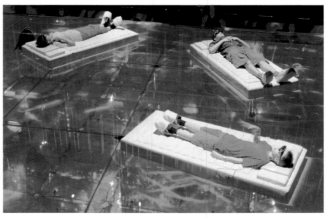

GRAFFITI RESEARCH LAB

LASER TAG
Rotterdam, Netherlands, 2007

The New York-based Graffiti Research Lab is dedicated to providing graffiti artists with open-source technologies for urban communication. In its simplest form, the Laser Tag system is a camera and laptop setup which tracks a green laser point across the face of a building and generates graphics based on the laser's position, which then get projected back onto the building with a high-powered projector.

TROIKA

SMS GUERILLA PROJECTOR
London, United Kingdom, 2006

The SMS Guerrilla Projector by the London-based, multidisciplinary design consultancy TROIKA is a homemade, fully functioning device that enables the user to project SMS text messages in public spaces, in streets, onto people, inside cinemas, shops and houses. Small, portable and battery operated, the SMS Guerrilla Projector contains a mobile phone which enables the device to receive and project messages from other people. The device is made by recombining available technologies. As an open object, the projector generates a wide range of applications, allowing the user to display messages and share his reflections.

LEONARD VAN MUNSTER

BLIND POETRY
Moscow, Russia, 2006

For this project van Munster created the BeamMobile, a truck fitted with mobile projection equipment that creates temporary 'light graffiti' by beaming images onto large buildings, bridges and other physical structures. The project began in Moscow, where van Munster invaded public urban space, creating a temporary presence without damaging the buildings. Blind Poetry showed a random mix of camera zooms on words from censored Russian newspapers. In this way van Munster created poems with unpredictable meanings.

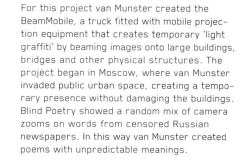

ONL (OOSTERHUIS_LÉNÁRD)
Kas Oosterhuis and Ilona Lénárd

MUSCLE
Paris, France, 2003

This project was realised as part of the Non-Standard Architecture exhibition at the Centre Pompidou in Paris, France. MUSCLE is a pressurised soft volume wrapped in a mesh of tensile 'muscles', which expand and contract by varying the air pressure pumped into them, to change length, height and width. MUSCLE is programmed to respond to human visitors. The public can play an interactive game with the MUSCLE via sensors attached to various reference points on the structure. These input devices convert the behaviour of the human players into data, which then act as parameters for changes in the physical shape of the active structure as well as the ambient soundscape.

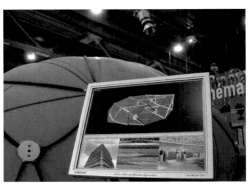

HYPERBODY RESEARCH GROUP
Delft University of Technology

MUSCLE BODY
Delft, Netherlands, 2005

JELLY ARCHITECTURE
Mishima, Japan, 2005

COLLEGE OF ENVIRONMENTAL DESIGN
University of California Berkeley

LIFEBEAN
Berkeley, USA, 2006

The LifeBean prototype was designed and built by students as part of a seminar course by Mark Anderson at the College of Environmental Design, University of California Berkeley, USA. It focuses on the relationships between building systems, designers and fabricators.

The LifeBean is a rapidly deployable emergency shelter and life-support system. It can be easily transported to disaster sites to offer immediate protection and longer-term support mechanisms for people caught in circumstances of infrastructural crisis. Designed to be transported by truck, plane, helicopter, or even by bicycle, its function as an immediate shelter can adapt to encompass semi-permanent habitation. To streamline the design process, team members derived the LifeBean's systemic logic from the efficient, sophisticated clarity of a green bean's structural, insulating, circulatory and enclosure mechanisms. Air bladders anchored within the LifeBean's double-layered skin interlock with rigid, bent bamboo ribs. Additional, interchangeable bladders store and filter water for human needs and thermal comfort. The whole integrated system regulates light, insulation, ventilation and access.

1 | **CONNECTOR**
New York, USA, 2004
2 | **ARCHITECTURE TRIENNIAL**
Oslo, Norway, 2004

TULLIN
Oslo, Norway, 2005

RAUMLABOR BERLIN

DER BERG
Berlin, Germany, 2005

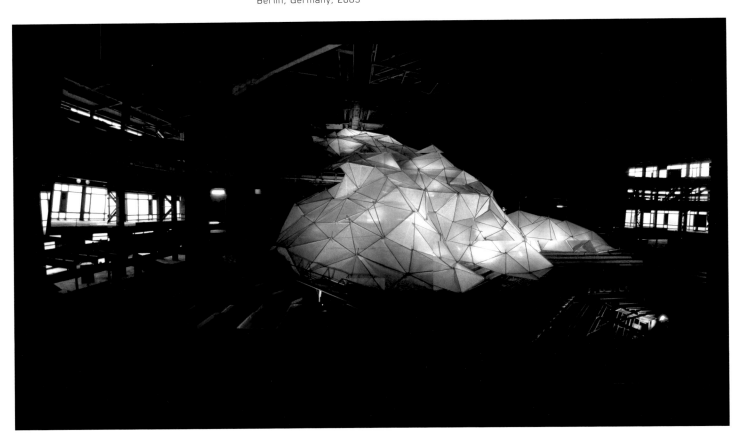

GAGAT INTERNATIONAL
Luc Merx

page 224 / 225 | **GARTENSAAL 05**
Würzburg, Germany, 2005

PLASTIQUE FANTASTIQUE
Marco Canevacci

1 | **BURBUJA MANCHEGA**
Castilla La Mancha, Spain, 2007
2 | **SAN SALVARIO MON AMOUR**
Turin, Italy, 2005
3 | **49TH IFHP WORLD CONGRESS**
Rome, Italy, 2005

PLASTIQUE FANTASTIQUE
Marco Canevacci

4 | **A2**
Munich, Germany, 2004

5 | **NITLAUS**
Barcelona, Spain, 2001

ART LEAGUE HOUSTON
Dan Havel, Dean Ruck

<u>INVERSION</u>
Texas, USA, 2005

B&K+ BRANDLHUBER & KNIESS
Arno Brandlhuber, Bernd Kniess

IN VITRO LANDSCAPE
Stuttgart, Germany, 1999

This project by the German architecture office b&k+ was realized as part of the exhibition in vitro landscape – Grundlagen zur Architekturgenetik 1 in the Weissenhof architecture gallery in Suttgart.

MIKAN ARCHITECTS

HANGER TUNNEL
Yokohama, Japan, 2005

LUIS RAFAEL BERRÍOS-NEGRÓN

NONSPHERES IV
Berlin, Germany, 2007

WINDSHAPE
Lacoste, France, 2006

Windshape was an ephemeral structure commissioned by the Savannah College of Art & Design, Atlanta, USA, as a gathering space for students and as a venue to host events on their French campus in Lacoste, Provence. Windshape became the main public meeting space in the small town, and hosted concerts, exhibitions and ceremonial gatherings throughout the summer. The project was designed by nARCHITECTS and built together with a team of students over a period of five weeks.

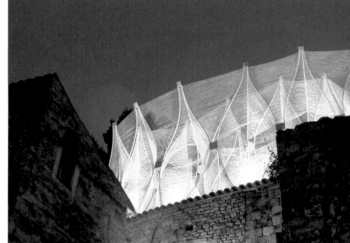

DETROIT COLLABORATIVE DESIGN CENTER
University of Detroit, Mercy School of
Architecture

FIRE BREAK
Detroit, USA, 2004 / 2005

The Detroit Collaborative Design Center is
a multidisciplinary teaching centre located
within the University of Detroit's Mercy School
of Architecture. It is dedicated to searching
and (re)searching architectural design, neighbourhood development and urban revitalisation
via the interaction of students, professionals,
faculty and community members.

The intent of the Fire Break project is to fabri-
cate and construct a series of installations in
and around burned and vacant houses on the
east side of Detroit with community artists
and residents. What motivates these artistic
actions is the intense desire to transform a
particular and distinct blight on the landscape
into an asset – a way of turning a negative
condition into a positive one.

MATEJ ANDRAŽ VOGRINIČIČ

1 | **DRESSED HOUSE**
Ljubljana, Slovenia, 1993
2 | **CASA VESTITA / DRESSED HOUSE**
Venice, Italy, 1999

For these projects, Slovenian artist Matej Andraž Vogrinčič dressed a house in his home town Ljublijana and on the popular Campo Santa Margherita in Venice, Italy with clothes donated from people living in the city. The installation process involved the adaptation of a huge stock of carefully chosen clothing, awnings and other materials for the project, as well as the dismantling and redistribution to friends and family of the constituent parts of the work afterwards. It also compared the layering effects of clothing with the layering effects of architectural structure and ornament. It focused attention on the ancient metaphor of the body in architecture, where walls are perceived as 'skin'.

LUIS RAFAEL BERRÍOS-NEGRÓN

VERDE QUE TE QUIERO VERDE
Kabul, Afghanistan, 2006

This project by Puerto Rican architect and artist Luis Rafael Berríos-Negrón resulted from a workshop with Afghan art students at the Centre for Contemporary Art in Afghanistan. The aim of the workshop was to use the artwork not only as an exercise in creative dialogue, but also as a pedagogical mechanism to apply performative technologies as tools for transformation. The intervention took place atop Bibi Mahro, a hill in the centre of Kabul. As a high point in the middle of the city, it is not only visually and culturally prominent, but also a strategic military site. The site has endured the traumatic history of Kabul, a fact that is underscored by the surrounding military debris. The students and the artist viewed the intervention as a contribution to the visual and emotional landscape of the city.

DANIEL DILGER, MARC OSWALD,
NIKLAS SCHECHINGER AND
HANK SCHMIDT IN DER BEEK

JA!
Offenbach / Main, Germany, 2003

1 | **NIGHTTOWN / LLIK**
Rotterdam, Netherlands, 2006
2 | **THE BLUE HOUSE**
Rotterdam, Netherlands, 2004

R&SIE(N)
Francois Roche

SNAKE
Paris, France, 2003

The white-skinned Snake by François Roche's Paris-based creative team R&Sie(n) is a design for the private gallery of an art collector in Paris.

DO-HO SUH

1 | **SEOUL HOME**
Los Angeles, USA, 1999

2 | **PERFECT HOME**
New York, USA, 2002

LOCO ARCHITECTS
Manabu + Nez / Loco

EXPERIMENTAL HOUSE
Tsukuba, Japan, 2005

THE SNOW SHOW
Carsten Höller / Tod Williams and
Billie Tsien

MEETING SLIDES
Sestriere, Italy, 2004

Originally conceived by independent curator Lance Fung in 2000, the Snow Show has
resulted in various structures that have
furthered the discussion of interdisciplinary
collaboration. The project explores art and
architectural issues by creating works from
the ephemeral materials of snow and ice. For
each piece, an internationally-acclaimed artist
was partnered with an architect, and they
were invited to develop a work together in a
dialogue that created a bridge between the
art and architectural worlds.

THE SNOW SHOW
Yoko Ono / Arata Isozaki

PENAL COLONY
Rovaniemi, Finland, 2004

DILLER SCOFIDIO + RENFRO

BLUR BUILDING
Yverdon-les-Bains, Switzerland, 2002

The Blur Building was an exhibition pavilion built for the Swiss Expo02 on Lake Neuchatel in the town of Yverdon-les-Bains. It was an architecture of atmosphere. The primary building material, water, is indigenous to the site. Water was pumped from the lake, filtered, and shot as a fine mist through a dense array of high-pressure mist nozzles. The resulting mass-produced fog was a dynamic interplay of natural and man-made forces. While not exactly a building, Blur was a habitable medium – one that is spaceless, formless, featureless, depthless, scaleless, massless, surfaceless and dimensionless.

HANS SCHABUS

ROB VOERMAN

INDEX

IMPRINT

SPACECRAFT
Fleeting Architecture and Hideouts

All texts written by Lukas Feireiss
Spacecraft was edited by Robert Klanten and Lukas Feireiss

Layout by Birga Meyer, Daniel Adolph & Mario Lombardo
Cover photo by Andy Ryan
Art direction by Robert Klanten
Project management by Julian Sorge for dgv
Production management by Martin Bretschneider for dgv
Translation and copy editing by Sophie Lovell
Proofreading by English Express, Berlin
Printed by Offsetdruckerei Grammlich, Pliezhausen

Published by Die Gestalten Verlag, Berlin 2007
ISBN 978-3-89955-192-1

RAUMTAKTIK

MIKE MEIRÉ

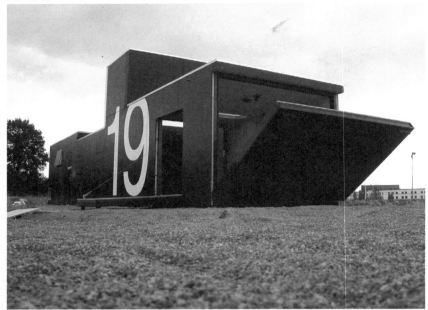

KORTEKNIE STUHLMACHER ARCHITECTEN

UCHRONIA